Developing Reading Strategies through Link

Text Connections

Bernadette Carroll
Melinda Derry
Maria Moran
Denise Savage
Nisha Tank

Series Editor: Bernadette Carroll

Pearson Education
Edinburgh Gate
Harlow
Essex
CM20 2JE

England and Associated Companies throughout the World

ISBN 0582 84865 2

First published 2004

Printed in China
NPCC/01

The Publisher's policy is to use paper manufactured from sustainable forests

Designed by Jackie Hill 320 Design

Picture Research by Ann Thomson

The cover photograph has been kindly supplied by Zefa Visual Media
UK Ltd

Sources and acknowledgements

Texts
We are grateful to the following for permission to reproduce copyright material:

Pat Ashworth for an extract concerning Ellen MacArthur by Pat Ashworth originally published in Derbyshire Life and Countryside; Avalon Management Group Ltd on behalf of Jenny Eclair for the article 'Driving Miss Daisy' as published in the AA Magazine summer 2003 © Jenny Eclair; BBC Wildlife Magazine for extracts from 'Tales from the Bush' by Adrian Hillman published in BBC Wildlife Magazine Vol 20, No 2 February 2002 and 'Clever, or what' by Mike Beynon published in BBC Wildlife Magazine Vol 21, No 6 June 2003; Casarotto Ramsay & Associates Limited for an extract from Educating Rita © Willy Russell 1985. All rights whatsoever in this play are strictly reserved and application for performance etc, must be made before rehearsal to Casarotto Ramsay & Associates Ltd, National House, 60-66 Wardour Street, London W1V 4ND. No performance may be given unless a licence has been obtained; dooyoo.co.uk Ltd for an extract concerning Kefalonia published on www.dooyoo.co.uk; Eland Books for an extract from The Road to Nab End by William Woodruff; Faber and Faber Limited for the poem 'Going, Going' by Philip Larkin; Geographical for an extract from 'In search of the true explorer' by Benedict Allen published in Geographical December 2002 © Geographical, the Magazine of the Royal Geographical Society; The Independent for an extract from 'Dilemma Virginia Ironside' as published in The Independent; Jodrell Bank Observatory for the advert Explore the Universe by Dr Tim O'Brien; Kogan Page for an extract from 'What a sports nutritionist does' published in Great Careers for People Interested in Sports and Fitness by Joanna Griffs; Macmillan Publishers for an extract from The Machine Gunners by Robert Westall; Mainstream Publishing Co. (Edinburgh) Ltd for an extract from Playground of the Gods by Ian Stafford; Florence McNeil for the poem 'First Dive'; Microsoft for the advert Unleash the wrath of the gods from Age of Mythology © Microsoft Corporation; Mountain Beach for an extract from 'Hidden Greece' published in Mountain Bike Holidays in Greece and France 1999; Penguin Group (UK) for Tribes by Catherine Macphail published by Puffin © Catherine Macphail 2001; PFD for an extract from Whose Side are you on? by Martyn Forrester; The Random House Group Limited and Judith Murdoch Literary Agency for an extract from Dance with a Poor Man's Daughter by Pamela Jooste published by Black Swan; Anthony Swift for an extract from 'Kumar's story' by Anthony Swift published in New Internationalist July 1997 © Anthony Swift; Time Warner Books Group for an extract from Long Walk to Freedom by Nelson Mandela.

We have been unable to trace the owners of some copyright material and would appreciate any information that would enable us to do so.

Photographs
We are grateful to the following for permission to reproduce copyright photographs:

Corbis for pages 146 (top left), 148; Getty images for pages 145, 146 (middle left), 146 (right), 149 (right), 149 (left), 152; Photodisc for pages 113, 114, 117-118, 119, 120, 121, 129, 130, 131, 132, 133, 134, 136, 137; Hartmut Schwarzbach/Still Pictures for pages 146 (bottom left), 151; Richard Taylor Jones/BBC Wildlife magazine for pages 114 (top left), 115.

Contents

Introduction

Reading

Text Connections 11–14 supports the teaching of reading, and this remains an important focus within the wider study of English in a number of ways:

- Reading should be taught explicitly. Pupils need to understand what good readers do and develop their ability to orchestrate a variety of reading strategies.
- Improving reading has an impact on writing and speaking and listening. Improvement in reading equips pupils with the knowledge of text types that is a vital step towards improvement in writing. Similarly, pupils can use their reading skills to interpret meanings in spoken texts, become more focused listeners and apply their awareness of text types to develop an understanding of spoken forms.
- The National Curriculum specifies a range of reading and pupils need access to interesting and challenging texts across a wide variety of genres, both fiction and non-fiction that will help them develop as independent readers for pleasure as well as confident readers of texts across the curriculum.
- Formal assessment at Key Stage 3 involves a separate assessment of reading.

Text Connections 11–14 is a whole key stage reading resource which develops pupils' ability in reading by:

- Systematically teaching a wide range of reading strategies based on the NATE/DfES model. Once familiar with these, pupils can select and combine them according to the demands of the text as they develop into good readers.
- Providing texts that match National Curriculum reading requirements and which are linked by theme. This thematic organisation familiarises pupils with the format of the various formal assessments in Key Stage 3.
- Covering a range of Framework objectives for reading in Y7, Y8 and Y9. In addition, others at word, sentence and text level writing are included where relevant.
- Matching Framework objectives to the QCA reading Assessment Focuses so that there is an explicit link between the teaching and learning and the assessment of reading.

Pupils' Book

The Text Connections 11–14 Pupils' Book contains 16 units, each on a different theme. The units are organised for progression through the key stage starting from level 4 in the early units up to level 7 in the later units, but each can also be adapted for a range of abilities. In each unit there is a set of three linked texts with a sequence of activities for each text which explicitly teaches different reading strategies and types of reading.

The Pupils' Book also contains explanations of the reading strategies for pupils to refer to either independently or as directed by the activities (pages 7–8). Pupils should be encouraged to use this list as a quick reference whenever they need to remind themselves of the explanations. In addition, the Pupils' Book provides a list of the four types of reading (skimming, scanning, close reading and continuous reading) with explanations of when and how pupils should use each of these provided. Specific instructions about the type of reading required are given each time pupils are ask to read a text. Worksheets listing the reading strategies are also provided in the Teacher's File on pages 13–15 and these can be photocopied for pupil reference.

Each unit in the Pupils' Book is organised as follows:

- Each unit begins with a summary of the theme of the unit which explains the way the texts are linked. These aim to engage the interest of pupils and could also provide initial discussion points, an opportunity to gauge prior learning or reading experience or predict elements of the theme or text types included.
- Reading strategies are then listed. This focuses pupils on a manageable number of strategies that they will use during the unit and provide an opportunity to revise them before applying them to the texts in the unit.
- A pre-reading activity is given in each unit to focus pupils' attention on a particular reading strategy. These could be used as starter activities.

- Context information for each individual text is then explained. These provide pupils with brief details that set the texts in their time and place and, where extracts have been used, identify the wider context of the whole text. They also relate the texts to experiences with which pupils are likely to be familiar and prepare them for the reading they are about to do.
- Activities are grouped under headings based on the QCA Assessment Focuses and are written in pupil-friendly language. This means that a link is made between the Framework objectives that the activities teach and the assessment of those skills. They also help to explain to pupils the type of response that the activity requires.
- The activities are designed to build understanding of each text and lead to a compare task that focuses on two or three of the group of texts. Two, or sometimes three, aspects of the text have been chosen for detailed work so that there is a manageable focus for pupils. The activities vary in demand and length: choose to do all for each text or select from among them.
- The activities have been designed to be possible to complete by pupils from the Pupils' Book without additional resources. Therefore, the instruction will often be to make a list or complete a table. Pupils could be provided with additional materials to help them to annotate or sequence, for example, or with whiteboards or OHTs to add variety to the approaches used.

Teacher's File

The Text Connections 11–14 Teacher's File supports the Pupils' Book by providing comprehensive support for the teaching of a key text or task in each unit, focusing on one of more of the activities from the Pupils' Book. This support consists of medium-term plans, lesson plans, guided reading planners, group worksheets and annotated texts. This support demonstrates the lesson structures and ways of working with texts that teachers can apply to other texts and activities in each unit.

CD-ROM

The Text Connections CD-ROM provides comprehensive support for teachers. It contains:

- The Teacher's File in PDF format.
- Lesson plans, guided reading planners and group worksheets in an editable format.
- Annotated texts of every text from the Pupils' Book. These texts are interactive, allowing annotations to be switched on and off by the teacher making them ideal for use with interactive whiteboards and during shared reading sessions.
- Full mark schemes for each practice test are provided enabling teachers to identify areas of strengths and weaknesses in pupils' reading.

Medium-term plan

- This page provides teachers with a summary of the key teaching and learning focuses of the unit.
- Reading strategies that are taught in the unit are listed. This provides a quick reference point for teachers and a reminder to build in the teaching of these when planning the lessons.
- The relevant QCA reading assessment focuses for the unit are listed and matched to framework objectives from across the key stage which are given in short name tag form. The framework objectives are grouped under each assessment focus and the chart on pages 9–12 shows how these are covered by each unit.

Sample lesson plan

- The lesson plan focuses on a specific text and activity in the Pupils' Book, and these are referenced at the beginning of the lesson plan. It shows how the activities can be selected, developed and adapted into complete lessons.

- The assessment focuses and framework objectives for the lesson are stated, with the links between them made clear. Teachers will need to select the appropriate objectives for their class as the objectives listed cover the key stage. Note that there is not a direct equivalent for every objective in every year of the Framework and with some pupils, teachers may wish to choose objectives from a different year.

- The lesson plan has a four-part lesson structure, with approximate timings. Depending on the class, more or less time will need to be spent on different activities in the lesson. The way in which the four-part structure supports the teaching of reading strategies is detailed below.

- Suggestions are made for differentiation as well as some suggested answers and examples to use with pupils. The activities in the Pupils' Book do offer support and examples to make the activities accessible to a range of pupils while still remaining appropriately challenging. They can also be customised in various ways, based on knowledge of the class and the needs of individual pupils.

- Resources: the lessons do not demand many additional resources, but an OHT copy of a section of text is sometimes needed for modelling so that the class can focus on a shared copy and to allow text marking to be demonstrated. Other classroom staples like mini-whiteboards will contribute towards the interactivity of the sessions.

The four-part structure supports and scaffolds the teaching and learning of specific reading strategies and skills in the following ways:

- Starter: These short, active sessions are focused on exploring the relevant reading strategy and/or framework objectives.

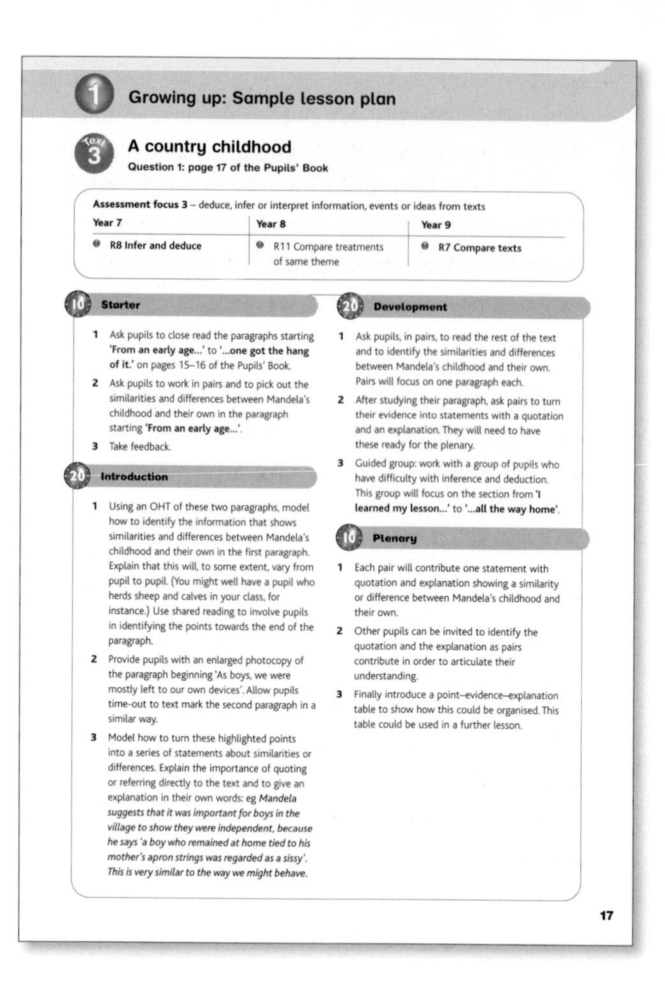

1 Growing up: Sample lesson plan

Text 3 A country childhood

Question 1: page 17 of the Pupils' Book

Assessment focus 3 – deduce, infer or interpret information, events or ideas from texts

Year 7	Year 8	Year 9
R8 Infer and deduce	R11 Compare treatments of same theme	R7 Compare texts

10 **Starter**

1 Ask pupils to close read the paragraphs starting **'From an early age...'** to **'...one got the hang of it.'** on pages 15–16 of the Pupils' Book.
2 Ask pupils to work in pairs and to pick out the similarities and differences between Mandela's childhood and their own in the paragraph starting **'From an early age...'**.
3 Take feedback.

20 **Introduction**

1 Using an OHT of these two paragraphs, model how to identify the information that shows similarities and differences between Mandela's childhood and their own in the first paragraph. Explain that this will, to some extent, vary from pupil to pupil. (You might well have a pupil who herds sheep and calves in your class, for instance.) Use shared reading to involve pupils in identifying the points towards the end of the paragraph.
2 Provide pupils with an enlarged photocopy of the paragraph beginning 'As boys, we were mostly left to our own devices'. Allow pupils time-out to text mark the second paragraph in a similar way.
3 Model how to turn these highlighted points into a series of statements about similarities or differences. Explain the importance of quoting or referring directly to the text and to give an explanation in their own words: eg *Mandela suggests that it was important for boys in the village to show they were independent, because he says 'a boy who remained at home tied to his mother's apron strings was regarded as a sissy'. This is very similar to the way we might behave.*

20 **Development**

1 Ask pupils, in pairs, to read the rest of the text and to identify the similarities and differences between Mandela's childhood and their own. Pairs will focus on one paragraph each.
2 After studying their paragraph, ask pairs to turn their evidence into statements with a quotation and an explanation. They will need to have these ready for the plenary.
3 Guided group: work with a group of pupils who have difficulty with inference and deduction. This group will focus on the section from **'I learned my lesson...'** to **'...all the way home'**.

10 **Plenary**

1 Each pair will contribute one statement with quotation and explanation showing a similarity or difference between Mandela's childhood and their own.
2 Other pupils can be invited to identify the quotation and the explanation as pairs contribute in order to articulate their understanding.
3 Finally introduce a point–evidence–explanation table to show how this could be organised. This table could be used in a further lesson.

17

- Introduction: The use of teacher demonstration or modelling before shared reading is a key part of each lesson. The annotated texts will provide information to support the modelling and text marking. Within the introduction, shared reading then develops, with time-out for pupils to try for themselves before sharing as a class.

- Development: Pupils work independently in a variety of different groupings. Some suggestions for differentiation are given. A group work sheet is provided to support pupils working independently. Guided reading takes place during this time, and is also supported by a separate plan. A summary of the guided task is given in the main lesson plan. Often, the focus of this work is the same as for the whole group, but tailored to meet the needs of the ability group selected. For example, they might explore a different piece of text or look at a section in more detail.

- Plenary: This is an opportunity for the different groups to share their learning and for the teacher to assess the progress made. It specifically revisits the framework objectives and the reading strategies pupils have been working on. This is sometimes a whole class session, but can also involve group discussions or individual self-assessment.

Guided reading planner

- A separate planner for guided reading is included. The link with the activity in the Pupils' Book, the assessment focuses and framework objectives is repeated so it is to hand which ever lesson plan the teacher is referring to during the lesson.
- The plan for the session follows a common standard sequence: introduction to the text; strategy check; independent reading and related task; return to the text, developing the response; review. For further information about running guided reading see the DfES Standards site www.standards.dfes.gov.uk/keystage3.
- Important features include the focus on the reading strategy and the time for independent reading. The sessions are generally 20-25 minutes, so teachers will need to move quickly through the plan.

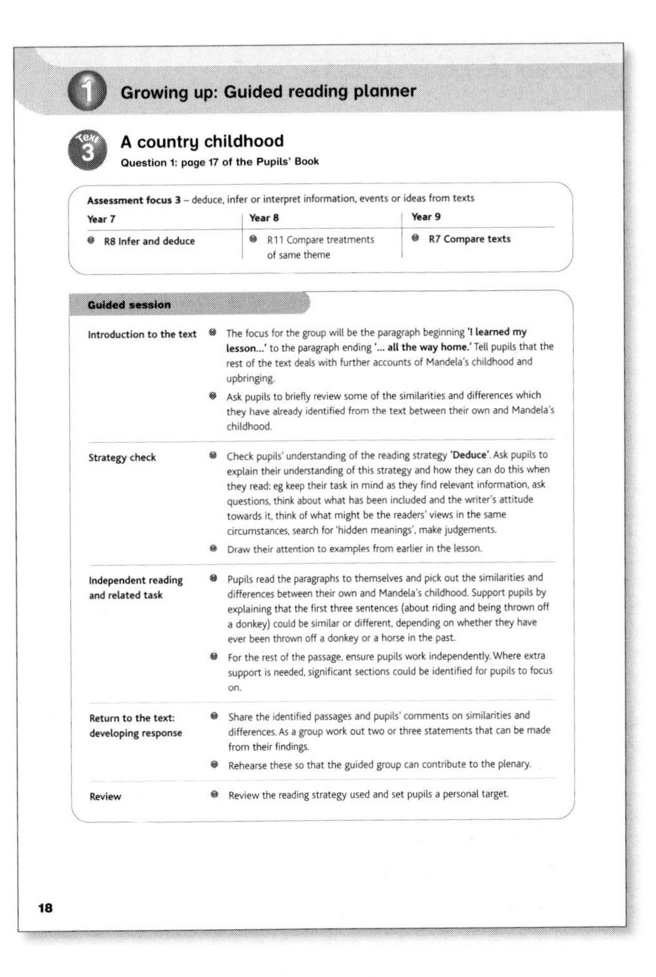

1 Growing up: Guided reading planner

Text 3 A country childhood

Question 1: page 17 of the Pupils' Book

Assessment focus 3 – deduce, infer or interpret information, events or ideas from texts

Year 7	Year 8	Year 9
R8 Infer and deduce	R11 Compare treatments of same theme	R7 Compare texts

Guided session

Introduction to the text	• The focus for the group will be the paragraph beginning **'I learned my lesson...'** to the paragraph ending **'... all the way home.'** Tell pupils that the rest of the text deals with further accounts of Mandela's childhood and upbringing. • Ask pupils to briefly review some of the similarities and differences which they have already identified from the text between their own and Mandela's childhood.
Strategy check	• Check pupils' understanding of the reading strategy **'Deduce'**. Ask pupils to explain their understanding of this strategy and how they can do this when they read: eg keep their task in mind as they find relevant information, ask questions, think about what has been included and the writer's attitude towards it, think of what might be the readers' views in the same circumstances, search for 'hidden meanings', make judgements. • Draw their attention to examples from earlier in the lesson.
Independent reading and related task	• Pupils read the paragraphs to themselves and pick out the similarities and differences between their own and Mandela's childhood. Support pupils by explaining that the first three sentences (about riding and being thrown off a donkey) could be similar or different, depending on whether they have ever been thrown off a donkey or a horse in the past. • For the rest of the passage, ensure pupils work independently. Where extra support is needed, significant sections could be identified for pupils to focus on.
Return to the text: developing response	• Share the identified passages and pupils' comments on similarities and differences. As a group work out two or three statements that can be made from their findings. • Rehearse these so that the guided group can contribute to the plenary.
Review	• Review the reading strategy used and set pupils a personal target.

18

Group worksheet

- A worksheet is provided to support the rest of the class while the guided session is underway. This contains information about the reading strategies pupils should use, as well as the framework objectives and a reminder of the work done up to this point in the lesson.
- The task is explained with appropriate hints to enable pupils to work without direct supervision. This helps them to remember what they are doing and know what is expected of them by the end of the lesson.

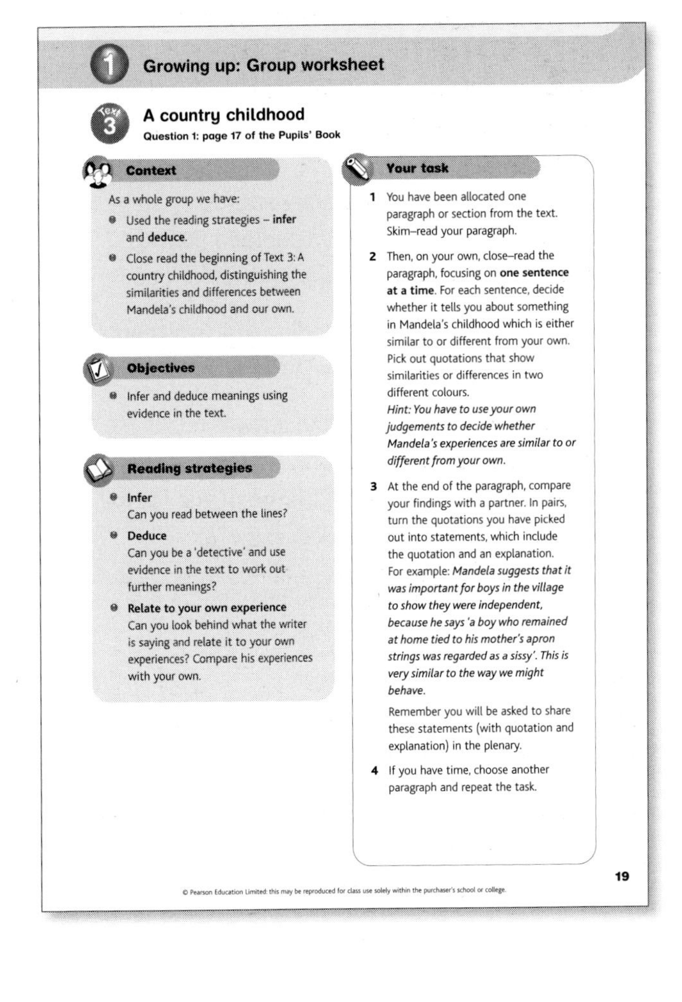

1 Growing up: Group worksheet

Text 3 A country childhood

Question 1: page 17 of the Pupils' Book

Context

As a whole group we have:

- Used the reading strategies – **infer** and **deduce**.
- Close read the beginning of Text 3: A country childhood, distinguishing the similarities and differences between Mandela's childhood and our own.

Objectives

- Infer and deduce meanings using evidence in the text.

Reading strategies

- **Infer**
  Can you read between the lines?
- **Deduce**
  Can you be a 'detective' and use evidence in the text to work out further meanings?
- **Relate to your own experience**
  Can you look behind what the writer is saying and relate it to your own experiences? Compare his experiences with your own.

Your task

1 You have been allocated one paragraph or section from the text. Skim–read your paragraph.

2 Then, on your own, close–read the paragraph, focusing on **one sentence at a time**. For each sentence, decide whether it tells you about something in Mandela's childhood which is either similar to or different from your own. Pick out quotations that show similarities or differences in two different colours.
Hint: You have to use your own judgements to decide whether Mandela's experiences are similar to or different from your own.

3 At the end of the paragraph, compare your findings with a partner. In pairs, turn the quotations you have picked out into statements, which include the quotation and an explanation.
For example: *Mandela suggests that it was important for boys in the village to show they were independent, because he says 'a boy who remained at home tied to his mother's apron strings was regarded as a sissy'. This is very similar to the way we might behave.*
Remember you will be asked to share these statements (with quotation and explanation) in the plenary.

4 If you have time, choose another paragraph and repeat the task.

19

© Pearson Education Limited: this may be reproduced for class use solely within the purchaser's school or college.

Annotated text

- Key information relevant to the activities in the Pupils' Book is given in the annotations, highlighting word, sentence and text level features of the text.
- Saves preparation time as it can be used as reference during shared reading and modelling sessions.
- Can be used as a handout to reinforce textual features for pupils after these have been identified during reading.
- All of the texts from the Pupils' Book are available electronically on the CD-ROM.

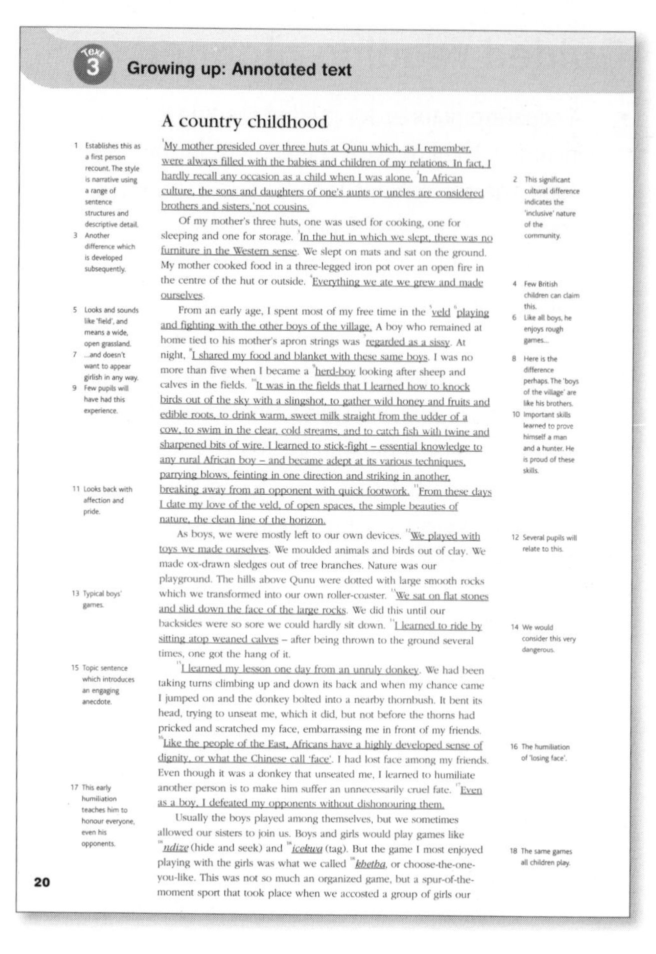

Text 3 Growing up: Annotated text

A country childhood

[1]My mother presided over three huts at Qunu which, as I remember, were always filled with the babies and children of my relations. In fact, I hardly recall any occasion as a child when I was alone. [2]In African culture, the sons and daughters of one's aunts or uncles are considered brothers and sisters, not cousins.

Of my mother's three huts, one was used for cooking, one for sleeping and one for storage. [3]In the hut in which we slept, there was no furniture in the Western sense. We slept on mats and sat on the ground. My mother cooked food in a three-legged iron pot over an open fire in the centre of the hut or outside. [4]Everything we ate we grew and made ourselves.

From an early age, I spent most of my free time in the [5]veld [6]playing and fighting with the other boys of the village. A boy who remained at home tied to his mother's apron strings was [7]regarded as a sissy. At night, [8]I shared my food and blanket with these same boys. I was no more than five when I became a [9]herd-boy looking after sheep and calves in the fields. [10]It was in the fields that I learned how to knock birds out of the sky with a slingshot, to gather wild honey and fruits and edible roots, to drink warm, sweet milk straight from the udder of a cow, to swim in the clear, cold streams, and to catch fish with twine and sharpened bits of wire. I learned to stick-fight – essential knowledge to any rural African boy – and became adept at its various techniques, parrying blows, feinting in one direction and striking in another, breaking away from an opponent with quick footwork. [11]From these days I date my love of the veld, of open spaces, the simple beauties of nature, the clean line of the horizon.

As boys, we were mostly left to our own devices. [12]We played with toys we made ourselves. We moulded animals and birds out of clay. We made ox-drawn sledges out of tree branches. Nature was our playground. The hills above Qunu were dotted with large smooth rocks which we transformed into our own roller-coaster. [13]We sat on flat stones and slid down the face of the large rocks. We did this until our backsides were so sore we could hardly sit down. [14]I learned to ride by sitting atop weaned calves – after being thrown to the ground several times, one got the hang of it.

[15]I learned my lesson one day from an unruly donkey. We had been taking turns climbing up and down its back and when my chance came I jumped on and the donkey bolted into a nearby thornbush. It bent its head, trying to unseat me, which it did, but not before the thorns had pricked and scratched my face, embarrassing me in front of my friends. [16]Like the people of the East, Africans have a highly developed sense of dignity, or what the Chinese call 'face'. I had lost face among my friends. Even though it was a donkey that unseated me, I learned to humiliate another person is to make him suffer an unnecessarily cruel fate. [17]Even as a boy, I defeated my opponents without dishonouring them.

Usually the boys played among themselves, but we sometimes allowed our sisters to join us. Boys and girls would play games like [18]*ndize* (hide and seek) and [18]*icekwa* (tag). But the game I most enjoyed playing with the girls was what we called [18]*khetha*, or choose-the-one-you-like. This was not so much an organized game, but a spur-of-the-moment sport that took place when we accosted a group of girls our

1 Establishes this as a first person recount. The style is narrative using a range of sentence structures and descriptive detail.
2 This significant cultural difference indicates the 'inclusive' nature of the community.
3 Another difference which is developed subsequently.
4 Few British children can claim this.
5 Looks and sounds like 'field', and means a wide, open grassland.
6 Like all boys, he enjoys rough games...
7 ...and doesn't want to appear girlish in any way.
8 Here is the difference perhaps. The 'boys of the village' are like his brothers.
9 Few pupils will have had this experience.
10 Important skills learned to prove himself a man and a hunter. He is proud of these skills.
11 Looks back with affection and pride.
12 Several pupils will relate to this.
13 Typical boys' games.
14 We would consider this very dangerous.
15 Topic sentence which introduces an engaging anecdote.
16 The humiliation of 'losing face'.
17 This early humiliation teaches him to honour everyone, even his opponents.
18 The same games all children play.

20

Assessment

- Three practice reading tests for use in years 7, 8 and 9 are provided.
- Papers developed by an experienced key stage 3 marker to ensure that the texts and themes chosen are suitable and appropriate for pupils.
- Reinforce pupils' understanding of assessment focuses with expertly developed test questions.
- Separate reading papers and answer booklets can be photocopied and provided to pupils to familiarise them with the format of the formal assessment of reading in key stage 3.
- Full mark schemes for each practice test are provided on the CD-ROM

Framework matching chart

1 Growing up

Assessment focus	Year 7	Year 8	Year 9
AF2	**R2** R4	R3 R5	R1 R3
AF3	R6 **R8**	R4 R11	**R7**
AF5	R14	R7	**W7** **R7**

2 Emergencies

Assessment focus	Year 7	Year 8	Year 9
AF2	**R2**		R1
AF3	**R2** R8	R7	**W7**
AF4	R7	**R5**	
AF5	**R12** R14	W11	**R12**

3 Healthy eating?

Assessment focus	Year 7	Year 8	Year 9
AF2	R1 **R2**	R1	R1 **R2**
AF4	**Sn13** R3 R7	R8 **R10**	Wr12
AF5	R13 R14	Sn9	W6 R7

4 Saving animals

Assessment focus	Year 7	Year 8	Year 9
AF1	W14 W16	W7a W7b W7c	
AF2	**R2**	**R2**	R1
AF5	**R12** R14	W11 R11	**R12**
AF6	R6	R4 **R5** R11	R11

Framework matching chart

5 Sport

Assessment focus	Year 7	Year 8	Year 9
AF2	R1 **R2**	R1	R1 **R2**
AF5	**R12** R14	W11 W12 R7	W6 R7

6 The world of work

Assessment focus	Year 7	Year 8	Year 9
AF3	R6 R8 **S&L15**	R4 R7 R11 S&L15	**W7** R1 S&L12
AF5	W16 R14	W11 **W14** R7	**R7** **R12**
AF6	R9 R16	**R5** R11	R3 R6

7 Discoveries

Assessment focus	Year 7	Year 8	Year 9
AF3	**R8** R18	R7	**W7**
AF5	**R12** R14	W11 W12 R7	**R7** **R12** R14
AF6	R9 R16	**R5** R11	R6 **R11**

8 Rituals

Assessment focus	Year 7	Year 8	Year 9
AF2	**R2** R4	**R2** R3	R1 R3
AF3	**R8**	R7	**W7** **R7**
AF5	**R12** R14	**R10**	**R7**

Framework matching chart

9 Violent Earth

Assessment focus	Year 7	Year 8	Year 9
AF4	R7 R15	**R10**	**R7**
AF5	R13 R14	W11 R7	**R7**
AF6	R9	**R5** R6 R11	R6 R11

10 Islands

Assessment focus	Year 7	Year 8	Year 9
AF2	R2 R4 R6	R2 R3 R4	R1 R3
AF4	R7 R13	**R10**	**Sn6** **R7**
AF5	R13 R14	R7	**W7**

11 Aliens and UFOs

Assessment focus	Year 7	Year 8	Year 9
AF3	**R8**	R7	**W5**
AF4	R7 R10	R8 **R10**	R7
AF5	R14	R7 R10	**W7** R12
AF6	R9	**R5** R11	R11

12 Food, glorious food

Assessment focus	Year 7	Year 8	Year 9
AF2	R2 R4	**R2** R3	R1 R3
AF3	**R8**	R7	**W7**
AF4	R7	**R10**	W8 **R7**
AF5	R14	W11 **R10**	**R12**

Framework matching chart

13 New worlds

Assessment focus	Year 7	Year 8	Year 9
• **AF3**	• R8 • R9	• R7 • R8	• W7
• **AF4**	• R7	• **R5** • R10	• **R7**
• **AF6**	• R9 • R16	• R6 • R11	• R11

14 Moving about

Assessment focus	Year 7	Year 8	Year 9
• **AF2**	• **R2**	• **R2**	• R1
• **AF3**	• **R8**	• R7	• **W7**
• **AF5**	• R3 • R14	• W12 • R7 • R11	• R7 • **R12**
• **AF6**	• R9	• **R5** • R6 • R11	• R11

15 Heroes

Assessment focus	Year 7	Year 8	Year 9
• **AF3**	• R6 • **R8**	• R4 • R7 • R11	• **W7** • **R7**
• **AF4**	• R7	• **R10** • Sn7	• **R7** • **Sn6**
• **AF5**	• R14	• R7	• R7

16 Places worth saving

Assessment focus	Year 7	Year 8	Year 9
• **AF3**	• R6 • **R8**	• R4 • R6 • R7	• W7 • R4
• **AF5**	• **R12** • R14	• W11 • R14	• **R12**
• **AF6**	• R16	• R11	• R6 • R10 • R11
• **AF7**	• R19	• R16	• **R16**

Reading strategies

See images

- Visualise what the writer is describing. What pictures can you see of the characters, the settings and the action?
- Ask others about their mental pictures and tell them about yours. Are they the same?

Predict what will happen

- Weather forecasts use facts and prior knowledge to predict the weather. Use what you know about a text to suggest what you think will happen next.
- Can you explain why? What evidence have you got?

Establish a relationship with the narrator

- Think about the narrator – the person telling you the information in the text. Identify who the narrator is. Do you like her/him? What would you say to her/him if she/he were in the room now?

Make judgements

- What do you **really** think? Share your opinion of the characters, the settings and the events with others. Do you like them? If not, why not? Did your opinions change as you read more?

Speculate

- Gaze into that crystal ball! What do you see? What do you think could happen in the end? Think of as many different possibilities as you can.
- Share your speculations with others and see whether you agree or not.

Rationalise what is happening

- Step outside the text and look on the events as a detached observer, like a reporter.
- Think logically about the characters or people, what they do and what happens to them. Does everything make sense? If not, why not?

Establish a relationship with the writer

- Can you hear the writer's voice? Is the author hiding behind a narrator or character or speaking directly to the reader?
- What do you think the writer is trying to say to you?

Feel

- Try and feel what the characters or people are feeling in the situation that they are in. What do you want to happen to them?
- What feelings does the writer want you to have about the characters and what is happening?

Reading strategies

Empathise

- Imagine you are in the same situation as the characters or people. What would you do? How would you feel?

Infer

- Look for what is being implied rather than made explicit. Read between the lines to find the meaning.
- The choice of words and how they are organised are ways writers can suggest different meanings.

Reinterpret

- As you read, consider how your ideas about the people and events in the text are changing.
- Do you feel and think the same as you did at the beginning? With more information your reaction might now be different.

Deduce

- Be a detective. Use evidence in the text to work out what is meant. You might have to fill some gaps and make links between ideas.

Relate to your own experience

- Does this remind you of anything you have done in your life or anything you have seen or heard about?
- How does this make you feel about the events in the text?

Read backwards and forwards

- Think of this as a chance to rewind and fast-forward. Clarify your understanding by making links back to what you have just read and forward to what is coming next.

Relate to previous reading experience

- Compare what you are reading with other texts that you have read. In what ways is it similar or different?
- What features of this type of text do you recognise or expect to see?

Re-read

- Can you spot anything new that you didn't see before?
- Try to deepen your understanding as you become more familiar with the text.

Reading strategies

Hear a reading voice

- As you read, think about whose voice you are hearing and how it changes through the story. Imagine it being spoken on the radio or in a live performance.
- Think about how the central characters sound and the sound effects of all the action. What can you hear while you read?

Interpret patterns

- Think about how the characters are linked. What are the similarities and differences between them? Can you group some of them together? And if so, what does each group represent?
- Think about how the events are linked. Are they random or are they leading somewhere in particular?

Ask questions

- Ask yourself questions all the time: who, why, what, where, when, how? Why do the characters do what they do? Why did that event happen and why did it happen in that way?
- Ask yourself why the writer has written the text in this way. What is the significance of the details the author includes? Do the details mean something?

1 Growing up

Introduction

The texts in this unit explore how childhood experiences help to shape the person that we become in later life and examine the different pressures that young people can face as they grow up.

The first week

What sort of person are you?

A country childhood

Reading strategies

- hear a reading voice
- infer
- relate to your own experience
- empathise
- make judgements
- deduce

Assessment focuses and framework objectives

Select the appropriate objectives for your class from the lists below, grouped by assessment focus. Consider not just their year group but also their starting point for this aspect of reading and the desired focus for the teaching.

Assessment focus 2 – understand, describe, select or retrieve information, events or ideas from texts and use quotation and reference to text

Year 7	Year 8	Year 9
• **R2 Extract information** • R4 Note-making	• R3 Note-making formats • **R5 Trace developments**	• R1 Information retrieval • R3 Note-making at speed

Assessment focus 3 – deduce, infer or interpret information, events or ideas from texts

Year 7	Year 8	Year 9
• R6 Active reading • **R8 Infer and deduce**	• R4 Versatile reading • R11 Compare treatments of same theme	• **R7 Compare texts**

Assessment focus 5 – explain and comment on writers' uses of language including grammatical and literary features at word and sentence level

Year 7	Year 8	Year 9
• R14 Language choices	• R7 Implied and explicit meanings	• **W7 Layers of meaning** • **R7 Compare texts**

A country childhood

Question 1: page 17 of the Pupils' Book

Assessment focus 3 – deduce, infer or interpret information, events or ideas from texts

Year 7	Year 8	Year 9
R8 Infer and deduce	R11 Compare treatments of same theme	R7 Compare texts

Starter

1. Ask pupils to close read the paragraphs starting **'From an early age…'** to **'…one got the hang of it.'** on pages 15–16 of the Pupils' Book.
2. Ask pupils to work in pairs and to pick out the similarities and differences between Mandela's childhood and their own in the paragraph starting **'From an early age…'**.
3. Take feedback.

Introduction

1. Using an OHT of these two paragraphs, model how to identify the information that shows similarities and differences between Mandela's childhood and their own in the first paragraph. Explain that this will, to some extent, vary from pupil to pupil. (You might well have a pupil who herds sheep and calves in your class, for instance.) Use shared reading to involve pupils in identifying the points towards the end of the paragraph.
2. Provide pupils with an enlarged photocopy of the paragraph beginning 'As boys, we were mostly left to our own devices'. Allow pupils time-out to text mark the second paragraph in a similar way.
3. Model how to turn these highlighted points into a series of statements about similarities or differences. Explain the importance of quoting or referring directly to the text and to give an explanation in their own words: eg *Mandela suggests that it was important for boys in the village to show they were independent, because he says 'a boy who remained at home tied to his mother's apron strings was regarded as a sissy'. This is very similar to the way we might behave.*

Development

1. Ask pupils, in pairs, to read the rest of the text and to identify the similarities and differences between Mandela's childhood and their own. Pairs will focus on one paragraph each.
2. After studying their paragraph, ask pairs to turn their evidence into statements with a quotation and an explanation. They will need to have these ready for the plenary.
3. Guided group: work with a group of pupils who have difficulty with inference and deduction. This group will focus on the section from **'I learned my lesson…'** to **'…all the way home'**.

Plenary

1. Each pair will contribute one statement with quotation and explanation showing a similarity or difference between Mandela's childhood and their own.
2. Other pupils can be invited to identify the quotation and the explanation as pairs contribute in order to articulate their understanding.
3. Finally introduce a point–evidence–explanation table to show how this could be organised. This table could be used in a further lesson.

A country childhood

Question 1: page 17 of the Pupils' Book

Assessment focus 3 – deduce, infer or interpret information, events or ideas from texts

Year 7	Year 8	Year 9
R8 Infer and deduce	R11 Compare treatments of same theme	**R7 Compare texts**

Guided session

Introduction to the text	• The focus for the group will be the paragraph beginning **'I learned my lesson...'** to the paragraph ending **'... all the way home.'** Tell pupils that the rest of the text deals with further accounts of Mandela's childhood and upbringing. • Ask pupils to briefly review some of the similarities and differences which they have already identified from the text between their own and Mandela's childhood.
Strategy check	• Check pupils' understanding of the reading strategy **'Deduce'**. Ask pupils to explain their understanding of this strategy and how they can do this when they read: eg keep their task in mind as they find relevant information, ask questions, think about what has been included and the writer's attitude towards it, think of what might be the readers' views in the same circumstances, search for 'hidden meanings', make judgements. • Draw their attention to examples from earlier in the lesson.
Independent reading and related task	• Pupils read the paragraphs to themselves and pick out the similarities and differences between their own and Mandela's childhood. Support pupils by explaining that the first three sentences (about riding and being thrown off a donkey) could be similar or different, depending on whether they have ever been thrown off a donkey or a horse in the past. • For the rest of the passage, ensure pupils work independently. Where extra support is needed, significant sections could be identified for pupils to focus on.
Return to the text: developing response	• Share the identified passages and pupils' comments on similarities and differences. As a group work out two or three statements that can be made from their findings. • Rehearse these so that the guided group can contribute to the plenary.
Review	• Review the reading strategy used and set pupils a personal target.

Growing up: Group worksheet

A country childhood

Question 1: page 17 of the Pupils' Book

Context

As a whole group we have:

- Used the reading strategies – **infer** and **deduce**.
- Close read the beginning of Text 3: A country childhood, distinguishing the similarities and differences between Mandela's childhood and our own.

Objectives

- Infer and deduce meanings using evidence in the text.

Reading strategies

- **Infer**
  Can you read between the lines?
- **Deduce**
  Can you be a 'detective' and use evidence in the text to work out further meanings?
- **Relate to your own experience**
  Can you look behind what the writer is saying and relate it to your own experiences? Compare his experiences with your own.

Your task

1. You have been allocated one paragraph or section from the text. Skim-read your paragraph.
2. Then, on your own, close-read the paragraph, focusing on **one sentence at a time**. For each sentence, decide whether it tells you about something in Mandela's childhood which is either similar to or different from your own. Pick out quotations that show similarities or differences in two different colours.
   Hint: You have to use your own judgements to decide whether Mandela's experiences are similar to or different from your own.
3. At the end of the paragraph, compare your findings with a partner. In pairs, turn the quotations you have picked out into statements, which include the quotation and an explanation.
   For example: *Mandela suggests that it was important for boys in the village to show they were independent, because he says 'a boy who remained at home tied to his mother's apron strings was regarded as a sissy'. This is very similar to the way we might behave.*

   Remember you will be asked to share these statements (with quotation and explanation) in the plenary.
4. If you have time, choose another paragraph and repeat the task.

Text 3

Growing up: Annotated text

A country childhood

[1]My mother presided over three huts at Qunu which, as I remember, were always filled with the babies and children of my relations. In fact, I hardly recall any occasion as a child when I was alone. [2]In African culture, the sons and daughters of one's aunts or uncles are considered brothers and sisters, not cousins.

Of my mother's three huts, one was used for cooking, one for sleeping and one for storage. [3]In the hut in which we slept, there was no furniture in the Western sense. We slept on mats and sat on the ground. My mother cooked food in a three-legged iron pot over an open fire in the centre of the hut or outside. [4]Everything we ate we grew and made ourselves.

From an early age, I spent most of my free time in the [5]veld [6]playing and fighting with the other boys of the village. A boy who remained at home tied to his mother's apron strings was [7]regarded as a sissy. At night, [8]I shared my food and blanket with these same boys. I was no more than five when I became a [9]herd-boy looking after sheep and calves in the fields. [10]It was in the fields that I learned how to knock birds out of the sky with a slingshot, to gather wild honey and fruits and edible roots, to drink warm, sweet milk straight from the udder of a cow, to swim in the clear, cold streams, and to catch fish with twine and sharpened bits of wire. I learned to stick-fight – essential knowledge to any rural African boy – and became adept at its various techniques, parrying blows, feinting in one direction and striking in another, breaking away from an opponent with quick footwork. [11]From these days I date my love of the veld, of open spaces, the simple beauties of nature, the clean line of the horizon.

As boys, we were mostly left to our own devices. [12]We played with toys we made ourselves. We moulded animals and birds out of clay. We made ox-drawn sledges out of tree branches. Nature was our playground. The hills above Qunu were dotted with large smooth rocks which we transformed into our own roller-coaster. [13]We sat on flat stones and slid down the face of the large rocks. We did this until our backsides were so sore we could hardly sit down. [14]I learned to ride by sitting atop weaned calves – after being thrown to the ground several times, one got the hang of it.

[15]I learned my lesson one day from an unruly donkey. We had been taking turns climbing up and down its back and when my chance came I jumped on and the donkey bolted into a nearby thornbush. It bent its head, trying to unseat me, which it did, but not before the thorns had pricked and scratched my face, embarrassing me in front of my friends. [16]Like the people of the East, Africans have a highly developed sense of dignity, or what the Chinese call 'face'. I had lost face among my friends. Even though it was a donkey that unseated me, I learned to humiliate another person is to make him suffer an unnecessarily cruel fate. [17]Even as a boy, I defeated my opponents without dishonouring them.

Usually the boys played among themselves, but we sometimes allowed our sisters to join us. Boys and girls would play games like [18]*ndize* (hide and seek) and [18]*icekwa* (tag). But the game I most enjoyed playing with the girls was what we called [18]*khetha*, or choose-the-one-you-like. This was not so much an organized game, but a spur-of-the-moment sport that took place when we accosted a group of girls our

1 Establishes this as a first person recount. The style is narrative using a range of sentence structures and descriptive detail.

2 This significant cultural difference indicates the 'inclusive' nature of the community.

3 Another difference which is developed subsequently.

4 Few British children can claim this.

5 Looks and sounds like 'field', and means a wide, open grassland.

6 Like all boys, he enjoys rough games...

7 ...and doesn't want to appear girlish in any way.

8 Here is the difference perhaps. The 'boys of the village' are like his brothers.

9 Few pupils will have had this experience.

10 Important skills learned to prove himself a man and a hunter. He is proud of these skills.

11 Looks back with affection and pride.

12 Several pupils will relate to this.

13 Typical boys' games.

14 We would consider this very dangerous.

15 Topic sentence which introduces an engaging anecdote.

16 The humiliation of 'losing face'.

17 This early humiliation teaches him to honour everyone, even his opponents.

18 The same games all children play.

own age and demanded that each select the boy she loved. Our rules dictated that the girl's choice be respected and once she had chosen her favourite, she was free to continue on her journey escorted by the lucky boy she loved. [19]But the girls were nimble-witted – far cleverer than we doltish lads – and would often confer among themselves and choose one boy, usually the plainest fellow, and then tease him all the way home.

19 He learns a salutary lesson: that girls can be much more manipulative and cruel than boys.

[20]The most popular game for boys was *thinti*, and like most boys' games it was a youthful approximation of war. Two sticks, used as targets, would be driven firmly into the ground in an upright position about a hundred feet apart. The goal of the game was for each team to hurl sticks at the opposing target and knock it down. We each defended our own target and attempted to prevent the other side from retrieving the sticks that had been thrown over. As we grew older, we organized matches against boys from neighbouring villages and those who distinguished themselves in these fraternal battles were greatly admired, as generals who achieve great victories in war are justly celebrated.

20 The African version of a war game.

After games such as these, I would return to my mother's kraal where she was preparing supper. Whereas my father once told stories of historic battles and heroic Xhosa warriors, [21]my mother would enchant us with Xhosa legends and fables that had come down from numberless generations. These tales stimulated my childish imagination, and usually contained some moral lesson.

21 The oral tradition of storytelling is important in his culture.

Like all Xhosa children, I acquired knowledge mainly through observation. [22]We were meant to learn through imitation and emulation, not through questions. When I first visited the homes of whites, I was often dumbfounded by the number and nature of questions that children asked their parents – and their parents' unfailing willingness to answer them. In my household, questions were considered a nuisance; adults imparted such information as they considered necessary.

22 A major difference. African children, unlike European children, continue the traditional ways without asking questions.

The schoolhouse consisted of a single room, with a Western-style roof, on the other side of the hill from Qunu. I was seven years old, and on the day before I was to begin, my father took me aside and told me that I must be dressed properly for school. Until that time, I, like all the other boys in Qunu, had worn only a blanket, which was wrapped round one shoulder and pinned at the waist. My father took a pair of his trousers and cut them at the knee. He told me to put them on, which I did, and they were roughly the correct length, although the waist was far too large. My father then took a piece of string and drew the trousers in at the waist. I must have been a comical sight, but I have never owned a suit I was prouder to wear than my father's cut-off trousers.

From *Long Walk to Freedom* by Nelson Mandela

2 Emergencies

Introduction

These texts consider three very different kinds of emergencies and explore how people react and cope in these dangerous situations.

 Air raid  Volcanoes  Snow shelters

Reading strategies

- re-read
- relate to previous reading experience
- make judgements
- infer
- feel
- see images
- speculate
- ask questions

Assessment focuses and framework objectives

Select the appropriate objectives for your class from the lists below, grouped by assessment focus. Consider not just their year group but also their starting point for this aspect of reading and the desired focus for teaching.

Assessment focus 2 – understand, describe, select or retrieve information, events or ideas from texts and use quotation and reference to text

Year 7	Year 8	Year 9
R2 Extract information		R1 Information retrieval

Assessment focus 3 – deduce, infer or interpret information, events or ideas from texts

Year 7	Year 8	Year 9
R2 Extract information **R8 Infer and deduce**	R7 Implied and explicit meanings	**W7 Layers of meaning**

Assessment focus 4 – identify and comment on the structure and organisation of texts, including grammatical and presentational features at text level

Year 7	Year 8	Year 9
R7 Identify main ideas	**R5 Trace developments**	

Assessment focus 5 – explain and comment of writers' uses of language, including grammatical and literary features at word and sentence level

Year 7	Year 8	Year 9
R12 Character, setting and mood R14 Language choices	W11 Figurative vocabulary	**R12 Rhetorical devices**

Emergencies: Sample lesson plan

Air raid

Question 1: page 22 of the Pupils' Book

Assessment focus 3 – deduce, infer or interpret information, events or ideas from texts

Year 7	Year 8	Year 9
• **R8 Infer and deduce**	• R7 Implied and explicit meanings	• **W7 Layers of meaning**

Assessment focus 5 – explain and comment on writer's use of language, including grammatical and literary features at word and sentence level

Year 7	Year 8	Year 9
• **R12 Character, setting and mood** • R14 Language choices	• W11 Figurative vocabulary	• **R12 Rhetorical devices**

Starter

1 Refer pupils to the following reading strategies:

- **re-read**
- **speculate**
- **ask questions**

2 Read the first three paragraphs of the text aloud expressively. Then **ask the following questions**:

- I wonder why Westall began the chapter with Chas's name?
- Why does the writer repeat **'black, white'**?
- What kind of a noise would **'crush'** your eardrums?
- Is Chas the leader or is Cem taking the lead at this point?
- What does Cem mean by **'theirs'**?

Ask pupils to look back at the strategies and to identify which you were using as you read the text.

Introduction

1 Explain you are now going to use these three reading strategies to work out the first part of the answer to question 1: how Chas's relationship with Cem and Audrey makes it clear to the reader that Chas is the leader of the group. Present the text from *"What shall we do?" 'whispered Audrey'* to *'No-one'll think of looking there.'* Highlight Audrey's question, the verb *'whispered'*, the use of the imperative *'take'*, the adverb *'brutally'* and the alliteration in the last sentence.

Then **ask pupils the following questions:**

- Why does Audrey whisper? Does this tell us anything about her relationship with Chas?
- What sort of a word is **'take'**? What would Chas's tone of voice be at this point?
- What is 'brutal' about what Chas says?
- Why does Westall use alliteration to describe Audrey's departure?

2 Sum up for pupils what they now know about Chas's character from this conversation.

Development

1 Struggling readers will work as a guided group in this part of the lesson. Divide the remainder of the class into two groups. Ask one group to work on the second bullet point of question 1 and the other to work on the third bullet point. Instruct pupils to work in pairs in their groups.

Plenary

1 Ask pupils for the questions they still have about the text and list these on the whiteboard. Then list the following words and phrases on the whiteboard: 'maybe', 'might', 'perhaps', 'it could be' and 'possibly'. Explain to pupils that these are useful to use when **speculating**. Choose pupils to answer the questions listed, guiding them to answer the questions using the listed words and phrases.

Air raid

Question 1: page 22 of the Pupils' Book

Assessment focus 3 – deduce, infer or interpret information, events or ideas from texts

Year 7	Year 8	Year 9
• **R2 Extract information** • **R8 Infer and deduce**	• R7 Implied and explicit meanings	• **W7 Layers of meaning** • R1 Information retrieval

Assessment focus 5 – explain and comment on writers' uses of language, including grammatical and literary features at word and sentence level

Year 7	Year 8	Year 9
• **R12 Character, setting and mood** • R14 Language choices	• W11 Figurative vocabulary	• **R12 Rhetorical devices**

Guided session

Introduction to the text

- Ask pupils what they know about the character of Chas so far. What sort of a person is he and what words would best describe him? Ask them to provide evidence from the text to back up what they are saying.

Strategy check

- Remind pupils of the three reading strategies that they are using: Re-read (looking back at the text to find evidence you may not have noticed before, deepening your understanding of characters and events; Speculate (thinking of different interpretations, trying out ideas; Ask questions (why has the author included this detail, why do the characters do what they do?).
- Remind pupils of the focus question: how can we tell that Chas is the leader of the group?

Independent reading and related task

- Divide the group into pairs and give each pair one of the following sections of text to read:

  Pair 1: from *"What about us?' said Cem.'* to *'... lighting up the rooftops.'*
  Pair 2: from *"Go on!' screamed Chas.'* to *'... grabbed his shoulder.'*
  Pair 3: from *"Where the hell you been?"* to the end.
- Ask each pair to answer the following questions as they read:

  a Is Chas the leader here? How can you tell?

  b What questions do you still have about this section? (Ask pupils to write these down. They will refer to these in the plenary session.)

Return to the text: developing response

- Take responses to question **a**, asking pupils to return to the text to provide evidence for their answers. Model how to do this to support pupils.
- Encourage them to **re-read** the text and to **ask questions** when they don't understand. Draw attention to how different Chas is when with his father from how he is when with his friends. Model **speculating** why Westall chose the word **'squawked'** to describe Chas's voice at this point.

Review

- Discuss the instances in which it is helpful to use these reading strategies.

Emergencies: Group worksheet

Air raid

Question 1: page 22 of the Pupils' Book

Context

As a whole group we have:

- Begun to explore how the writer shows that Chas is the leader of the group by examining evidence from the text, focusing on his relationship with Cem and Audrey.

Objectives

- Find out information about characters using evidence from the text.

Reading strategies

- **Re-read**
  Can you spot anything new that you didn't see before? Try to deepen your understanding of the text
- **Make judgements**
  Share your opinions about the way Chas is shown to be the leader of the group. Do your opinions change as you read the passage?

Your task

1. Working in pairs, read from *'What about us?'* to the end of the text. Find out **either**:

   a What knowledge or information Chas has about the situation that they are in.

   or

   b What information we find out about Chas from the ways he talks to the others.

2. When you have completed your reading, look at the list below that applies to your question. Following the example given, complete the list by adding the information that you found out during the reading.

   Question a
   Information – He knows where the anti-aircraft guns are.

   Evidence – He thinks 'That was the guns at the castle.'

   Question b
   Information – Cem asks Chas what they should do.

   Evidence – Cem says 'What about us?' after Chas has sent Audrey home.

3. When you have completed your list, compare your responses with those of a pair who answered the other question. Discuss how the information you have found out helps you to answer the question of how the writer shows that Chas is the leader of the group.

Air raid

[1]Chas [2]despaired. And then suddenly the night turned [3]white, black, white, black, white. A [4]great hammer banged on the [5]dark tin tray of the sky, [6]crushing their ear-drums again and again. [7]Anti-aircraft guns. Then, in the following silence, came the noise of an aircraft engine.

[8]*Chug-chug-chug-chug*

'One of theirs,' whispered Cem. Then that [9]hammer was beating the sky again. Echoes of its blows rippled away, like someone slamming doors [10]further and further off down a corridor.

Chas stared at the sky, trying to guess where the next white flashes would come from. They came in, in a scattered pattern moving west. [11]Five at a time. [12]That was the guns at the Castle. Then a group of three together. That was the guns at Willington Quay.

[13]'What shall we do?' whispered Audrey.

'Take your bike and get to a shelter. We can manage without you.'

'But I shouldn't be out in the open during an air-raid.'

'You don't think these trees will shelter you from anything?' said Chas brutally. She [14]went, wobbling wildly across the waste ground.

'What about us?' said Cem.

'I'm getting this gun home while the streets are empty. This air-raid's the best chance [15]we got.'

'The wardens will stop us.'

'Not if we go by Bogie Lane.' Bogie Lane was a little-used cinder track that led through the allotments to near home. 'No one'll think of looking there.'

'Right, come on then.'

The blackness of night was back. As they dragged and bounced through the dark, the warning note of the air-raid siren sounded.

'Dozy swine. Caught asleep as usual,' said Cem in disgust.

'It's a sneak raider. They glide in without engines.'

'And he's hit something.' Cem nodded to the west, where a [16]rapidly growing yellow glare was lighting up the rooftops.

'Or else they got *him*. Must be Howdon way.'

'Only the one. All-clear will sound in a minute.'

But it didn't. They were halfway up Bogie Lane when they heard the *chug-chug-chug* of enemy engines again.

'More than one.'

'Six or seven.'

Ahead, the [17]night lit up as if great blue floodlights had been switched on. Blue points of light hung motionless in the sky, brighter than stars.

'They're dropping parachute flares.'

The *chug-chug-chug* grew nearer. They felt [18]like two small flies crawling across a white tablecloth. Up there, thought Chas, Nazi bomb-aimers were staring down through black goggles, teeth clenched, hands tight on bomb-release toggles, waiting for the cross-hairs of their bomb-sights to meet on Bogie Lane [19]and the two flies who crawled there.

[20]*Chug-chug-chug*. [21]Overhead now. They were safe, because bombs always dropped in a curve in front of bombers. He had watched them fall in newsreels of the Polish Campaign, out of black Stukas ...

1 Short sentence.
2 Strong verb.
3 Repetition.
4 Strong adjective.
5 Expanded noun phrase introducing metaphor
6 Verb used for impact.
7 Short phrase.
8 Onomatopoeia.
9 Repetition of metaphor.
10 Expanding the metaphor.
11 As if writer recording what children are hearing.
12 Reader drawn into the experience of the characters.
13 Dialogue breaking up description and showing character.
14 Alliteration.
15 Dialect.
16 Extended noun phrase.
17 Metaphor.
18 Simile.
19 Reader entering thoughts of character.
20 Onomatopoeia.
21 Short phrase.

[20]Bang, bang, bang. The hammer was at it again, right overhead. This meant a new danger: falling shell-shrapnel. Chas could hear it, [22]whispering and pattering down like steel rain all around.

20 Onomatopoeia.

22 Non-finite verbs.

'Go on!' screamed Chas. 'Get the bastards, kill the bastards!' Then silence, blackness, nothing. The parachute flares had gone out.

'Come on,' shouted Chas, dragging Cem to his feet. 'They'll be back in a minute.'

The bogie wheels crunched along the cinders, and they could hear the hard *knock, knock* of the machine-gun on the bogie's planks. They got back to the Square before trouble started again. A rough hand grabbed Chas's shoulder.

[23]'Where the hell you been?' It was his father, wearing a tin hat. 'Your mother's worried sick.'

23 Dialect.

'She knew I was going down Chirton,' squawked Chas.

'Get down the shelter. Who's that with you?'

'Cem.'

'Get him down as well. I'll go and tell his mother he's safe.'

'What about the Guy?'

Mr McGill dragged the bogie roughly against the garden hedge. 'It'll have to take its chance.'

From *The Machine Gunners* by Robert Westall

3 Healthy eating?

Introduction

These three texts consider the modern preoccupation with what we eat and what is or is not good for us. The texts explore the effects of junk food and also the vogue for healthy eating and examine how these issues are presented in texts and the ways these influence the reader.

Junk food addicts may sue

Diet 2000

Ice cream fat stuns scientists

Reading strategies

- ask questions
- interpret patterns
- relate to previous reading experience
- reinterpret

Assessment focuses and framework objectives

Select the appropriate objectives for your class from the lists below, grouped by assessment focus. Consider not just their year group but also their starting point for this aspect of reading and the desired focus for the teaching.

Assessment focus 2 – understand, describe, select or retrieve information, events or ideas from texts and use quotation and reference to text

Year 7	Year 8	Year 9
• R1 Locate information • **R2 Extract information**	• R1 Combine information	• R1 Information retrieval • **R2 Synthesise information**

Assessment focus 4 – identify and comment on the structure and organisation of texts, including grammatical and presentational features at text level

Year 7	Year 8	Year 9
• **Sn13 Stylistic conventions of non-fiction** • R3 Compare presentation • R7 Identify main ideas	• R8 Transposition • **R10 Development of key ideas**	• Wr12 Effective presentation of information

Assessment focus 5 – explain and comment on writers' uses of language, including grammatical and literary features at word and sentence level

Year 7	Year 8	Year 9
• R13 Non-fiction style • R14 Language choices	• Sn9 Adapting text types	• W6 Terminology for analysis • **R7 Compare texts**

Diet 2000

Questions 1–3: page 34 of the Pupils' Book

Assessment focus 4 – identify and comment on the structure and organisation of texts, including grammatical and presentational features at text level

Year 7	Year 8	Year 9
• **Sn13 Stylistic conventions of non-fiction** • R3 Compare presentation • R7 Identify main ideas	• R8 Transposition • **R10 Development of key ideas**	• Wr12 Effective presentation of information

Starter

1. Ask pupils to scan section 1 of the text, headed 'Breakfast', and identify any features of the layout which the writer uses to emphasise certain points.
2. Using an OHT of section 1, take feedback and annotate the text with the points noted by pupils. Discuss with the pupils how effective these devices are in helping to convey the advice to the reader.

Introduction

1. Using the OHT of section 1 of the text, do a shared reading of paragraph one with the pupils. Ask pupils to consider the kind of language the writer uses and where they might have seen this before. Draw pupils' attention to the writer's use of punctuation, verb tenses, noun phrases, pronouns etc and model marking and annotating the text for them.
2. In pairs, ask pupils to scan section 1 of the text again and pick out any imperative (commands) verbs which the writer uses to give advice to the reader. Take feedback and annotate the OHT. Discuss with pupils that these verbs are a feature of this kind of text and are accepted by the reader in spite of seeming to be 'bossy'. (See annotated version of the text on page 32.) Draw pupils' attention to any patterns in the use of different layout features or the use of imperative verbs in the text. Discuss with pupils possible reasons for these patterns.

Development

1. In threes, ask pupils to close read all three sections of the text and identify the key pieces of advice the writer gives about healthy eating. In their group of three ask pupils to focus on one section each then compare notes. Encourage pupils to think about how they decide whether one piece of advice is more key than another.
2. Ask pupils to record two pieces of key advice from each section on to a table ready to feedback in the plenary.

Plenary

1. Ask each group to contribute one piece of advice from their table and explain how the writer has used the language features explored in the introduction to deliver this advice to the reader.
2. Draw together the discussion by reminding the pupils of their objective and asking them to consider how effective the layout and language are in this advice text.

Diet 2000

Question 3: page 34 of the Pupils' Book

Assessment focus 4 – identify and comment on the structure and organisation of texts, including grammatical and presentational features at text level

Year 7	Year 8	Year 9
• **Sn13 Stylistic conventions of non-fiction** • R3 Compare presentation • R7 Identify main ideas	• R8 Transposition • **R10 Development of key ideas**	• Wr12 Effective presentation of information

Guided session

Introduction to the text

- Recap for understanding of the language features and layout used by the writer in section 1 of the text. Explain that in sections 2 and 3 the writer gives advice on 'Main Meals' and 'Snacks' in a similar way.

Strategy check

- Ask pupils to remember and explain the reading strategy '**Ask questions**'. Why has the author included one detail and not the other?
- Remind them to **question** why the writer has used particular words and techniques. If necessary, review the different questions that they might want to ask of the text, making the list available to them. Encourage pupils to be resourceful in their questioning of the text.
- Draw their attention to examples of the strategy from earlier in the lesson. Then share text marking of section 1 to model identifying key pieces of advice.
- How does the author's tone and choice of language affect the meaning?
- Does the style remind you of other things you've read and where?

Independent reading and related task

- Working in pairs, ask pupils to read sections 2 and 3 of the extract and identify two key pieces of advice the writer gives about healthy eating.
- Support pupils by helping them to identify all the pieces of advice in the section they are exploring and then helping them to sort these into order of importance.
- When each pupil has looked at the section they have chosen, ask them to compare notes within their pair.

Return to the text: developing response

- Share as a group the pieces of advice that pupils have found in each section. Discuss with pupils the way the writer has used the language and layout to emphasise this key advice to the reader. Make links with the examples found in section 1.

Review

- Invite the group to select one piece of advice from each section ('Main meals' and 'Snacks and light meals') of the text to feedback in the plenary. Review the reading strategies used and set personal targets.

Healthy eating?: Group worksheet

Diet 2000

Question 3: page 34 of the Pupils' Book

Context

As a whole group we have:

- Used the reading strategy – **ask questions**.
- Annotated the first section of Text 2: Diet 2000.
- Noted the features of the layout and the language the writer has used.

Objectives

- Recognise the conventions of an advice text.
- Identify and comment on the key points in a text and recognise how these are emphasised.

Reading strategies

- **Ask questions**
  Ask yourself why the author has written the text in this way. What is the significance of the details the author includes? Do the details mean something?

Your task

1 Skim read all three sections of the text and identify the key pieces of advice the writer gives about healthy eating. Work in groups of three and focus on one section each.

Hint: Think about the way the advice is presented in each section. The most important advice will often be emphasised through the use of presentational features.

2 Compare notes in your group and discuss the advice you have found. Do you agree or disagree with the advice your partners have selected as the key advice from their sections. Do you think any other pieces of advice are more important than the ones selected? Discuss your thoughts as a group and then record the key pieces of advice in a list, giving reasons for your choices.

3 Discuss the way the writer uses the layout and the language to deliver the advice to the reader in the section you looked at. Are there any similar features to those found by the other members of your group in the sections they looked at? Note down any patterns you can find and discuss possible reasons for these.

4 Remember your group will be asked to contribute one piece of advice from each section of the text to the summary in the plenary. Choose what you think is the most important advice from your section.

[1]Diet 2000

1. Breakfast

[2]Breakfast really is an essential meal. Skipping the first meal of the day [3]is one of the worst mistakes [4]you can make and this applies as much to slimmers as to those who are happy with their weight. If you miss out on breakfast you may not have eaten for 15 or 16 hours and [5]you will be lacking in energy by midday. [6]Concentration goes and headaches and irritability take over. [7]Start breakfast with a glass of freshly squeezed orange juice. [8]Then choose from a bowl of cereals[9]: [10]Swiss muesli with milk and fresh fruit; porridge or cooked oatbran; toast (wholemeal) thinly spread with butter; homemade muffins; French bread and apricot jam; Swedish baked rolls or crispbread. Add fresh fruit, skimmed milk or low-fat yogurt and [11]you'll have a really healthy start to the day.

[12]Hidden hazards

Check the labels on your breakfast cereals as they vary greatly in their sugar, salt and fibre content. High sugar and salt aren't necessarily a problem but it's useful to know what you are adding to the day's total.

- [13]**Salt**
  High content: Shredded Wheat, Weetabix
  Fairly high content: Puffed Wheat
- **Sugar**
  High content: Frosties, Crunchy Nut Cornflakes, Ricicles, Coco Pops, Sugar Puffs
  Fairly high content: All-Bran, Bran Buds, Bran Flakes, Sultana Bran, Oat Bran Flakes, Golden Crackles, Golden Oatmeal Crisps
- **Fibre**
  High content: All-Bran, Bran Buds
  Fairly high content: Weetabix, Shredded Wheat, Bran Flakes, Sultana Bran, Oat Bran Flakes

2. Main meals

The timing of your main meal, [14]if you have one, will depend on your lifestyle and the demands of [15]your job, leisure activities and family. You can use your main meal to fill in any nutritional gaps from the rest of the day. Make sure you have some protein-rich food if you've been eating salads and fruit all day. [16]Alternatively, add extra starchy food with plenty of fruit and vegetables [14]if you've been subsisting on fatty snacks and junk food.[17]

Here are some good menus for everyday healthy eating

- [18]Tomato soup with crusty rolls
- Ham and sweetcorn lasagne with green salad dressed with lemon juice
- Fruit kebabs

- Avocado with grapefruit
- Sesame chicken with stir-fry vegetables and rice
- Apricot yogurt

Annotations:

1 Heading in bold type and plain font: suggests serious topic.
2 Emphatic short statement – main piece of advice.
3 Use of the present tense.
4 Second person pronoun – personal. Direct appeal to the reader.
5 Emphasises the fact that this is a bad thing to do.
6 Statement of fact – paints a disturbing picture.
7 Use of imperative for instruction /advice.
8 Temporal connective to move the process up in logical steps.
9 Punctuation for effect – colon suggests lots of choices.
10 Expanded noun phrases to describe healthy options.
11 Modal verb to emphasise and predict the future – following this advice.
12 Not always obvious but things to look for when buying ingredients.
13 Bullet points, bold type and alliteration all emphasise key information.
14 Sentences linked by subordinating connective 'if'.
15 Use of the pronouns 'you' and 'your' to appeal directly to the reader on a personal level.
16 Adverb – textual connective for contrast.
17 Key pieces of advice personalise the advice and offers the reader choice.
18 Menus offer a range of choice appealing to different cultural tastes.

- Liver paté with toast
- Gujarati cabbage with rice and grilled tomatoes
- Fresh fruit

- Minestrone soup
- Jacket potatoes stuffed with mushrooms and bacon, green salad
- Peaches and ice-cream

- Bean and tuna salad
- Wholemeal pasta with pesto sauce
- Watercress and carrot salad with apples

3. Snacks and light meals

[19]As life gets more hectic, you tend to eat snacks more often. [20]There's nothing wrong with this. Provided you choose the right kind of food, a snack meal can be as healthy as any other.
Healthy snacks are sometimes seen as time-consuming to make [21]but a wholesome granary bread sandwich filled with tuna and salad takes no longer to make than a rather less healthy one filled with roast beef, lettuce and mayonnaise.
[22]When making sandwiches, slice the bread fairly thickly [23](it doesn't have to be doorsteps) and either omit the butter or margarine altogether or spread very thinly. Fill unbuttered pitta loaves or hollowed-out bread sticks for a change.

19 Adverbial phrases implies awareness of the pressures – not judgmental.

20 Clear emphatic statement. No guilt.

21 Coordinating connective gives the sub-clause equal weight here.

22 Use of imperative verbs again – the 'you' is understood and does not need to be stated. Still talking directly to the reader.

23 Colloquial language gives detail and makes the advice more personal.

Ideas for fillings

- [24]Liver paté or liver sausage and watercress.
- [25]Mixed grated Cheddar cheese and grated raw carrots. Toss the carrot in a little oil to stop it discolouring and losing its goodness.
- Sliced bananas and dates, moistened with a little lemon juice.
- Sliced mangoes layered with cottage cheese and mint.
- Finely chopped chicken mixed with chopped tomatoes and basil.
- Drained and mashed sardines mixed with a little vinegar and black pepper and layered with beetroot.

24 Bullet points used again for emphasis.

25 Verbs, adjectives and adverbs – technical vocabulary of recipes.

From *Diet 2000*

4 Saving animals

Introduction

The texts in this unit explore the relationships between humans and animals.

How much do you care about wildlife?

Turtle rescue

Zoos – the arguments

Reading strategies

- see images
- hear a reading voice
- feel
- re-read

Assessment focuses and framework objectives

Select the appropriate objectives for your class from the lists below, grouped by assessment focus. Consider not just their year group but also their starting point for this aspect of reading and the desired focus for the teaching.

Assessment focus 1 – use a range of strategies, including accurate decoding of text, to read for meaning

Year 7	Year 8	Year 9
• W14 Word meaning in context • W16 Unfamiliar words	• W7 a) Word families • W7 b) Unfamiliar words • W7 c) Words in context	

Assessment focus 2 – understand, describe, select or retrieve information, events or ideas from texts and use quotation and reference to text

Year 7	Year 8	Year 9
• **R2 Extract information**	• **R2 Independent research**	• R1 Information retrieval

Assessment focus 5 – explain and comment on writers' uses of language, including grammatical and literary features at word and sentence level

Year 7	Year 8	Year 9
• **R12 character, setting and mood** • R14 Language choices	• W11 Figurative vocabulary • R11 Compare treatments of same theme	• **R12 Rhetorical devices**

Assessment focus 6 – identify and comment on writers' purposes and viewpoints and the overall effect of the text on the reader

Year 7	Year 8	Year 9
• R6 Active reading	• R4 Versatile reading • **R5 Trace developments** • R11 Compare treatments of same theme	• R11 Author's standpoint

Saving animals: Sample lesson plan

Zoos – the arguments

Question 3: page 46 of the Pupils' Book

Assessment focus 5 – explain and comment on writers' uses of language, including grammatical and literary features at word and sentence level

Year 7	Year 8	Year 9
• R14 Language choices	• W11 Figurative vocabulary	• **R12 Rhetorical devices**

Assessment focus 6 – identify and comment on writers' purposes and viewpoints and the overall effect of the text on the reader

Year 7	Year 8	Year 9
• R6 Active reading	• R4 Versatile reading • **R5 Trace developments** • R11 Compare treatments of same theme	• R11 Author's standpoint

10 Starter

1 Think back to work done during this unit and the feelings that the texts have evoked in the pupils. Brainstorm a list of emotions that a writer could want a reader to **feel** about the events or ideas in a text. Alternatively, provide pupils with a list of words for them to categorise into positive and negative feelings. For example: surprised, confused, happy, sad, amazed, excited, shocked, worried, upset, concerned, anxious, angry, pleased, relieved.

15 Introduction

1 Focus on the first argument and display paragraph 1. Model effective reading aloud to persuade and express the intended meaning. Text mark to show how the reader might **feel** and how the writer achieves this.

2 Read the second paragraph aloud then give pupils time-out to discuss their feelings and how the writer encourages them. If necessary, support pupils by asking them to comment on the effect of words and phrases like 'wonderful', 'eavesdrop' and 'all round the world'. Take feedback and invite pupils to add these notes to the text.

Development

1 Focusing on the remainder of the text (or shorter sections for the lower attaining), have the pupils work in pairs to prepare a persuasive reading.

2 They should then note the **feelings** they have as readers and how the writer persuaded them to have those feelings. Support pupils by offering a series of prompts if necessary.

3 With a higher-attaining group, carry out guided reading focusing on the second argument. They should read the text aloud to draw attention to the persuasive techniques then explore, through close analysis of the text, how they respond as readers to the writer's techniques.

Plenary

1 Form groups of five or six, including one pupil from the guided group. They should share their persuasive reading of each text.

2 Pupils return to the list of emotions produced in the starter. Review the emotions felt by readers of these texts and the techniques used by the writers to produce those feelings in the reader.

Zoos – the arguments

Question 3: page 46 of the Pupils' Book

Assessment focus 5 – explain and comment on writers' uses of language, including grammatical and literary features at word and sentence level

Year 7	Year 8	Year 9
• **R12 Character, setting and mood** • R14 Language choices	• W11 Figurative vocabulary • R7 Implied and explicit meanings	• **R12 Rhetorical devices**

Assessment focus 6 – identify and comment on writers' purposes and viewpoints and the overall effect of the text on the reader

Year 7	Year 8	Year 9
• R6 Active reading	• **R5 Trace developments** • R11 Compare treatments of same theme	• R11 Author's standpoint

Guided session

Introduction to the text	• Model an initial reading to familiarise pupils with the content. • If pupils have read the text, remind them that the second argument opposes the statement about zoos being like prisons. Review the main arguments in the text and the images they could see.
Strategy check	• **Feel** – as they close read the text, pupils are going to think about how they feel. Remind them that the writer's words and ideas will affect them and they need to pause to think about how they **feel** and how the writer has made them feel like that. If necessary, review the different emotions that they might experience, making the list available to them. Encourage pupils to be precise in their description of their feelings.
Independent reading and related task	• Ask pupils to read the second argument independently, pausing to annotate a copy of the text with their feelings and the techniques used by the writer.
Return to the text: developing response	• Review the text as a group. Explore the different feelings noted by the readers and discuss how the writer created those feelings. • Note that this argument relies less on emotions and more on logic to convince the reader.
Review	• Discuss other texts where pupils could think about their feelings as they read (eg poetry, fiction) and those where the text is less likely to create an emotional response in the reader (eg fact/information texts, instructions).

Zoos – the arguments

Question 3: page 46 of the Pupils' Book

Context

As a whole group we have:

- Read part of the text aloud, making it sound persuasive.
- Discussed different emotions readers might feel as they read a text.
- Annotated the first two paragraphs of the text with our feelings as readers.
- Discussed how the writer has persuaded us to have those feelings.

Objectives

- Make sense of the text by actively thinking about and responding to it.
- Infer meanings from what a writer says.
- Explain how the writer's choice of words and sentences affects the reader.

Reading strategy

- **Feel**
  Think about how the text makes you feel. Be as precise as you can in identifying what your feelings are. Look at the way the text is written to see how the writer has managed to make you have that feeling.

Your task

1. Work in pairs. Read aloud the rest of the first argument about zoos, using expression and pace of reading to bring out the persuasive features.

   Hint: To do this well, you will need to be familiar with the text and read it confidently. You should each try reading different parts of the text. Give each other advice on how to improve the reading.

2. Close read the text. As you read, pause to consider **what** the writer is making you **feel**. Note down these feelings.

   Hint: Look back at the list you discussed in the starter if you need help.

3. Re-read the text, this time working out **how** the writer has created those feelings.

   Hint: Think about the techniques you have already discussed in the lesson. Are the same ones used here? Or is the writer using different techniques now?

4. Remember you might be asked to read aloud in the plenary and you will be asked to explain the notes you made about the text.

   If you have some spare time, rehearse your reading of the text.

Zoos – the arguments

[1]**Zoo Check**
Cherry Tree Cottage
Coldharbour
Dorking
Surrey RHS 6HA

Most young people have been to the zoo, taken there either by their parents or by their teacher. Perhaps you are one of them? If you are, your visit was probably described as a [2]'treat', a 'good day out', or a 'surprise'. But I wonder what you [3]**really** felt as you wandered round from [4]cage to cage?[5]

If you like nature and wildlife [6]I am sure you watch the [7]wonderful films we have on television nowadays, films that show you animals living in their natural environment. I am always amazed that, through television, I am now able to [8]eavesdrop on the lives of animals like the polar bear, the gorilla and the tiger – species from [9]all round the world.

[10]How does wildlife on television compare with the wildlife in the zoo? In the zoo do you see the polar bear hunting the vast icy wastes of the arctic for seals, or digging a 'snow cave' in which to raise its cubs? Do you watch the mother teaching her young how to survive in that harsh and difficult climate? Or do you see the [11]massive male silverback gorilla quietly leading his family through the African jungle, showing them which plants are good to eat, a watchful eye alert for any danger? Does the tiger in the zoo use its incredible camouflage to stalk its prey and then with a burst of speed race in for the kill?[12]

[13]What do you see and what do you learn at the zoo?[14]

All over the world wildlife needs [15]our help. Zoos say that they are vital centres for conserving animals that are threatened with extinction. [16]But though in the past 150 years zoos have [17]'saved' perhaps twenty species, we are now losing one species every day! So does the answer to the conservation crisis lie with the zoos? Or is the answer that [18]we – each of us – makes a pledge to help save the wild areas of the world and the huge variety of wildlife they contain without resorting to the unnatural captivity of the zoo? [19]The choice is ours.

Next time you go to the zoo, ask yourself three questions: Why am I here? Why are the animals here? And are zoos any more than outdated [20]prisons?

Perhaps we will never know, but I always wonder what the polar bear is thinking as it walks a few paces this way, a few paces that, its [21]horizon a blue-rinsed concrete wall, its ocean a small paddling pool, and its future an unfulfilled life of boredom in captivity.[22]

1 Address shows reader this argument is from a real organisation.

2 Inverted commas suggest these are the actual words but it could have a sarcastic tone.

3 'Really' is emphasised, suggesting you had different feelings.

4 Repetition of 'cage' makes it sound boring, monotonous, all the same. It also emphasises the fact that the animals are in cages while we are free to 'wander'.

5 Ends with a rhetorical question, provoking the reader to start thinking about what they did feel.

6 Suggests confidence that the reader does what the writer expects.

7 Persuades the reader to like the programmes and feel satisfied with them.

8 Sounds exciting and also far closer than you can get at a zoo.

9 Suggests TV films cover everything and that we should be satisfied with them. What more could we want?

10 These details make the reader appreciate animals in the wild revealing special moments and making us feel privileged.

11 Adjectives remind us how wonderful these animals are.

12 Make us dislike zoos because we have to answer 'no' to each question.

13 We feel guilty about justifying zoos as entertainment or education.

14 No answer is given to this question – you see and learn nothing worth mentioning.

15 It is now 'our' not 'you' and 'I'. The reader feels more included and responsible.

16 The efforts of zoos to save animals sound pathetic.

17 Inverted commas show that the writer doesn't really think zoos do much saving.

18 The writer spells out that 'us' includes the reader. Pause created by the dashes allows time for thought, for the meaning to sink in.

19 Short sentence at the end is blunt. Now it is our responsibility. We feel guilty.

20 This is emotive language.

21 Comparisons contrast zoo life with the wild.

22 Ends with three descriptions that remain in our minds.

Saving animals: Annotated text

23 Address establishes the writer of the argument: it will be in favour of zoos.

[23]**London Zoo**
Regent's Park
London NW1 4RY

24 Not most people – the writer wants us to feel differently.

25 Short abrupt sentence. We might be surprised and shocked out of the first viewpoint.

26 Compares us with animals. Expresses basic needs that we know zoos can provide.

27 Do we feel uneasy or are we reassured by the work of good zoos?

[24]Some people imagine that the only place animals should be seen is in the wild and that to keep them in zoos is cruel. [25]This is not true. [26]Like us, all animals have basic needs for food, water, shelter and security. They need to be able to exercise, explore their environment, behave normally, and be with other animals of their own kind when they want to be. Good zoos make [27]every effort to satisfy these requirements, while at the same time creating an environment where the animals are free from the stress of disease and predators.

28 Sounds like an obvious statement.

29 Contrasts good/bad zoos. Perhaps our objections are just about bad zoos.

30 Strong word.

31 List of three – sounds confident and convincing.

32 Comparison makes it sound like they do many impressive things.

33 Specific example of the good work of zoos.

34 Animals in the wild actually need zoos.

[28]Of course, not all zoos are the same. Keeping animals in [29]bad zoos is [30]inexcusable, but good zoos, where the animals are well taken care of, have a very valuable contribution to make to [31]science, conservation and education. Zoos such as London, New York, San Diego and Washington, for example, have large research programmes which [32]not only investigate animal behaviour and physiology, but also provide information and skilled personnel for projects in the wild. [33]Anaesthetic techniques developed for the Giant Panda at London Zoo, for example, make it possible to handle this rare animal safely in China. Zoos also support scientists in the field by paying their salaries or by providing them with training and technical expertise [34]essential to the success of the project in the wild.

35 Relief about a success story and perhaps guilt if we haven't heard of it.

36 More examples of good work. Zoos are reversing depopulation of the wild.

Zoos also contribute to the conservation of species. The [35]Arabian oryx was extinct in nature, but [36]thanks to a co-operative zoo breeding programme this beautiful antelope is now back in the wild in the deserts of Oman. Plans are now well under way for similar projects for other species of desert wildlife in Arabia and Africa.

37 Shows authority by mentioning unfamiliar animals. Perhaps we are more interested.

38 Emphasises the significance of these projects.

39 Mentions future (as did previous point of view).

The conservation of African rhinos, [37]Kouprey (a species of wild cattle), Partula snails and Asian arawana fish are all additional examples of [38]major international projects to combine the best of zoo-developed technology with programmes to save the species in the wild. The resources available from the zoos are vital to these projects [39]if they are to achieve their long-term aims.

40 Shatters the idealism of the previous article. Contrasts actual dangers with the relative safety of the zoo.

41 Ends with the suggestion that both sides are working to benefit animals.

[40]It is sadly true that less and less of the 'wild' exists now for the animals to live in. Even where there is the space, it may be impossible to protect them from hunters, starvation or loss of suitable habitat. [41]Zoos are not a replacement for nature, but they are a way of helping it to survive.

From *Whose side are you on?* by Michael Forrester

5 Sport

Introduction

The three texts in this unit use the topic of sport to explore the challenges that individuals face when trying to attain their ambitions.

Swimming against the tide

Bend It Like Beckham

First dive

Reading strategies

- see images
- hear a reading voice
- ask questions
- make judgements
- interpret patterns
- deduce

Assessment focuses and framework objectives

Select the appropriate objectives for your class from the lists below, grouped by assessment focus. Consider not just their year group but also their starting point for this aspect of reading and the desired focus for the teaching.

Assessment focus 2 – understand, describe, select or retrieve information, events or ideas from texts and use quotation and reference to text

Year 7	Year 8	Year 9
• R1 Locate information • **R2 Extract information**	• R1 Combine information	• R1 Information retrieval • **R2 Synthesise information**

Assessment focus 5 – explain and comment on writers' uses of language, including grammatical and literary features at word and sentence level

Year 7	Year 8	Year 9
• **R12 Character, setting and mood** • R14 Language choices	• W11 Figurative vocabulary • W12 Formality and word choice • R7 Implied and explicit meanings	• W6 Terminology for analysis • **R7 Compare texts**

Sport: Sample lesson plan

First dive

Questions 1–3: page 56 of the Pupils' Book

Assessment focus 5 – explain and comment on writers' uses of language, including grammatical and literary features at word and sentence level

Year 7	Year 8	Year 9
• R14 Language choices	• W11 Figurative vocabulary	• W6 Terminology for analysis

10 Starter

1. Read the poem aloud to the class and ask pupils to listen and think about how they are able to **hear the narrator's voice**. Discuss the poem with pupils and establish that the narrator is a young person preparing to make a first dive.
2. Working in pairs, ask pupils to skim read the poem and identify how the stanzas take us through the stages of the dive. Take feedback and model marking and annotating these stages on the text. (See the annotated text on page 42.)

Introduction

1. Using an OHT of the poem do a shared reading with the pupils. Work through the poem sharing and annotating to identify how the poet describes the contrast between the narrator and other divers. Draw out how the poet uses strong images and figurative language to convey the fear felt by the narrator as she stands on the board, anticipating the dive. (See the annotated text.)
2. Working in pairs, ask pupils to make a list of the words in the poem which describe the narrator and the other divers, eg **'the giants'**, **'a reluctant bird'**. Ask pupils to explain how the words show she is an inexperienced diver.

Development

1. Working in pairs, ask pupils to close read the poem to identify how the poet uses language to make the water and its surroundings seem threatening and terrifying to the narrator. Ask pupils to pick out key words and phrases from the text.
2. Then ask pupils to discuss the words and phrases they have selected. Encourage pupils to choose three powerful images used by the poet and explain the effects that these images have had on them as readers. Model a response to help pupils to prepare to feedback their responses in the plenary.
3. Guided group: work with a group needing further support.

Plenary

1. Take feedback from the class and annotate the OHT of the poem by highlighting the images they have selected.
2. Ask the class to comment on the quotations chosen and say how the writer has used strong images and figurative language to present the water as a terrifying place to the narrator. Ask pupils to think carefully about the impact of the writer's use of language on the reader. Where appropriate, encourage pupils to use the correct terminology when commenting on grammatical and literary features.

Sport: Guided reading planner

First dive

Questions 1–3: page 56 of the Pupils' Book

Assessment focus 5 – explain and comment on writers' uses of language, including grammatical and literary features at word and sentence level

Year 7	Year 8	Year 9
• R14 Language choices	• W11 Figurative vocabulary	• W6 Terminology for analysis

Guided session

Introduction to the text	• Set out the focus for the group: how the writer uses the language to make the water and its surroundings seem threatening to the narrator. Read the poem aloud for the pupils and model text marking and annotating the following example: '... the terrors/circulating quietly and steadily/under the surface'
Strategy check	• Ask pupils to check their understanding of the following reading strategies: • **See images** (Encourage pupils to visualise the events the poem describes. Ask pupils to build up a mental picture of the setting, the diver and the action as they read.) • **Ask questions** (Remind pupils of the different questions they can ask of the text: who, why, what, where, when and how? What is the significance of the different images the poet has chosen to include?) • **Infer** (Focus pupils on how the choice of words and how they are organised are ways in which writers can suggest different meanings.)
Independent reading and related task	• Ask pupils to read the second stanza again and pick out three images the poet has used to make the water sound frightening. Support pupils as they work through the poem choosing their images. Encourage pupils to think about which images have the most impact on them as a reader as they read.
Return to the text: developing response	• Share as a group the quotations pupils have selected from the second stanza of the poem. • Collect the images on a pupil whiteboard and then discuss with pupils what they think each image means. • Draw out how the poet has used words with strong connotations and powerful metaphors to make the narrator's fear of the water clear to the reader.
Review	• Ask the group to review their findings in pairs and choose one quotation and explanation to feedback in the plenary. • Review the reading strategies used and set personal targets.

First dive

Questions 1–3: page 56 of the Pupils' Book

Context

As a whole group we have:

- Used the reading strategies – **see images, ask questions** and **infer**.
- Made a list of the words that show the contrast between the narrator and the other divers.
- Noted the way the writer uses strong images and figurative language to convey the narrator's feelings.

Objectives

- Recognise the way the writer uses figurative language to create a frightening setting.

Reading strategies

- **See images**
  Have a picture of the setting and the action in your head. What do you see while you read? Ask others about their mental pictures and tell them about yours.
- **Ask questions**
  What is the significance of the details the author includes? Do the details mean something?
- **Infer**
  Read between the lines to find the meaning. What do the writer's choice of words and how they are organised suggest?

Your task

1. Skim read the poem again to remind yourself of the way the writer uses strong images to convey the writer's feelings about the dive.
2. Working in pairs, choose three images from the poem which show how the poet uses language to make the water and its surroundings seem threatening and terrifying to the narrator. Discuss the following example as a starting point:

   '........the terrors

   circulating quietly and steadily

   under the surface'

   Hint: What do you think the 'terrors' are? Why are they 'circulating quietly and steadily'? What do you usually associate with the word 'circulating'? Why do you think the writer has used the phrase 'under the surface'?
3. Discuss the images you have picked out with your partner. Explain what you think the poet is describing in each image. How does the writer's choice of words help to show the fear the narrator has of diving into the water?
4. Choose one image and write a brief explanation of the impact it has on you as a reader. Remember you will be asked to share this image and explanation in the plenary.

First dive

[1]Shivering in the hot August sun
[2] I [3]stand on the lowest diving board
[4]watching above me the giants
[5]fearlessly twist and knife
into [6]their dark waters

[7]I measure distance
in terms of
[8]multiple whales
and [9]weigh my eleven years
against [10]the terrors
[11]circulating quietly and steadily
under the surface
the [12]eyes that stare from green rocks
at [13]my naked feet
the [14]hands weaving seaweed nets
to complete the ambiguity
of my needless capture
a [15]surfeit of teeth and claws gathering
to oversee my [16]fate

[17]Reckless with fear
I become a wavering sigh
[18]a reluctant bird
lose head and hands and atmosphere
[19]to trespass suddenly
into [20]adult depths
[21]bobbing up transfigured victorious
out of an [22]unclaimed ocean.

By Florence McNeil

5 pr... the moves ... re experienced divers.

7 Stanza 2: confronting terrors that relate to what lies beneath the water – the terror of the ocean – whales/sharks – terrible images of death – narrator's fear of the water.

9 Balancing herself against the fear she feels – she feels very young.

11 Metaphor sounds like there are dangerous creatures beneath waiting to devour her.

13 She is vulnerable – unknown creatures live in the water.

15 Images of terror – teeth and claws – to underline her fear.

17 Fear makes her resigned to her fate – in spite of the terrors, almost cavalier.

19 Emphasis that she feels she has no right to be there.

21 Survives the dive and is transformed by a feeling of success – she has beaten fear and the dark ocean – almost like a religious experience, a baptism. 'Bobbing' suggests that it is the water in control of her body.

2 Use of first person – personal – involves the reader.

4 Contrast in size. She feels very small – like in a fairytale.

6 The other divers seem mysterious/fairy tale 'dark waters'.

8 Again emphasises the size of other drivers.

10 Unknown like 'their dark waters' – link back to first stanza.

12 Terrors personified

14 Fishermen working make her situation seem both ordinary and dangerous at the same time.

16 Inevitable.

18 Metaphor – the sensation of falling is like the sound of birds in flight – 'reluctant' because it isn't natural for a human being.

20 Usually only adults dive this deep.

22 The water remains powerful and apart from the diver – she has only entered it briefly.

The world of work

Introduction

These three texts illustrate different examples of working children past and present. They provide opportunities for pupils to empathise with the three examples and to reflect on current working conditions.

 Factory conditions in 1815

 We, the working children of the Third World

 A passion for print

Reading strategies

- deduce
- rationalise what is happening
- empathise
- read backwards and forwards
- ask questions
- establish a relationship with the writer
- speculate

Assessment focuses and framework objectives

Select the appropriate objectives for your class from the lists below, grouped by assessment focus. Consider not just their year group but also their starting point for this aspect of reading and the desired focus for the teaching.

Assessment focus 3 – deduce, infer or interpret information, events or ideas from texts

Year 7	Year 8	Year 9
• R6 Active reading • **R8 Infer and deduce** • **S&L15 Explore in role**	• R4 Versatile reading • R7 Implied and explicit meaning • R11 Compare treatments of same theme • S&L15 Work in role	• **W7 Layers of meaning** • R1 Information retrieval • S&L12 Drama techniques

Assessment focus 5 – explain and comment on writers' uses of language, including grammatical and literary features at word and sentence level

Year 7	Year 8	Year 9
• W16 Unfamiliar words • R14 Language choices	• W11 Figurative vocabulary • W14 Language change • R7 Implied and explicit meanings	• **R7 Compare texts** • **R12 Rhetorical devices**

Assessment focus 6 – identify and comment on writers' purposes and viewpoints and the overall effect of the text on the reader

Year 7	Year 8	Year 9
• R9 Distinguish writer's views • R16 Author attitudes	• **R5 Trace developments** • R11 Compare treatments of same theme	• R3 Note-making at speed • R6 Authorial perspective

The world of work: Sample lesson plan

A passion for print

Questions 1–3: page 65 of the Pupils' Book

Assessment focus 3 – deduce, infer or interpret information, events or ideas from texts

Year 7	Year 8	Year 9
• R6 Active reading • **R8 Infer and deduce**	• R4 Versatile reading • R7 Implied and explicit meaning	• R1 Information retrieval • **W7 Layers of meaning**

Starter

1. Ask pupils to re-read paragraphs five to seven starting '*Delivering newspapers taught me a lot about human nature...*' and, with a partner, start to create a bullet point list of things William Woodruff learned about people on his paper round.
2. Model how to do this by presenting the table from page 65 of the Pupils' Book on the whiteboard.
3. Get feedback from pupils. Make the point that these are his observations, but they also tell us what William Woodruff was like, even though it may not be explicitly stated. We have to play 'detective' and read between the lines to **deduce** that information.

Introduction

1. Using an OHT copy of paragraph five, model how to read between the lines in order to learn what the writer was really like. Use shared reading to involve pupils in identifying points. Invite them to text mark on the OHT. Make it clear that it is important to refer to the text to support your deductions.
2. Ask pupils to text mark paragraph six in a similar way.

Development

1. Explain that the class is going to build up a picture of what the writer was like from the whole text. Prepare a table on an OHT or a flip chart with two columns to show how information from the text can be used to **deduce** information about the writer.
2. Divide the class into three groups (this could be attainment groups, but there is room for flexibility). Divide the text into three sections and assign one of the sections to each of the groups. Pupils can work in pairs.
3. Explain that in the plenary, pupils will add to the table to create a class list of the writer's characteristics.
4. Guided group: work with a group of higher-attaining pupils. This group will focus on paragraphs one to four.

Plenary

1. Call pupils to the front of the class to contribute to the class table. Ask pupils to take it in turns to complete the 'Information from the text' column and then the 'What it tells us about the writer' column.
2. Fill in the obvious gaps by adding to the first column, and discussing with pupils what this tells us about the writer.
3. A further lesson could be spent developing these comments into a written response.

A passion for print

Question 1: page 65 of the Pupils' Book

Assessment focus 3 – deduce, infer or interpret information, events or ideas from texts

Year 7	Year 8	Year 9
• R6 Active reading • **R8 Infer and deduce**	• R4 Versatile reading • R7 Implied and explicit meaning	• R1 Information retrieval • **W7 Layers of meaning**

Guided session

Introduction to the text	• The group will focus on the first four paragraphs (from **'While we were living'** to **'...how my customers would vote'**). Explain that we learn much more about the writer from his descriptions and observations, but that we need to read between the lines to work out what he is like.
Strategy check	• Deduce – ask pupils to explain their understanding of this strategy and how they can do this when they read: eg keep their task in mind as they find relevant information, ask questions, think about what has been included and the writer's attitude towards it, think of what might be the readers' views in the same circumstances, search for 'hidden meanings', make judgements.
Independent reading and related task	• Ask pupils to read the four paragraphs independently. Support them by reading the first paragraph with them and reminding them how to make deductions about the writer (see the annotated text on page 47 for details). • Ask pupils to work in pairs to complete the table on 'Information from the text' and 'What it tells us about the writer'. Where extra support is needed, significant phrases could be picked out for pupils to focus on.
Return to the text: developing response	• Share feedback and discuss the writer's characteristics. Draw out the difference between the writer's observations of George and Madge Latham and the writer's observations about his own experiences. • As a group, summarise the points that could be made for the class table.
Review	• Review the reading strategy used and set a personal target.

The world of work: Group worksheet

A passion for print

Question 1: page 65 of the Pupils' Book

Context

As a whole group we have:

- Used the reading strategy – to **deduce** information.
- Annotated a section of the text and begun to make deductions about the author.
- Recorded our ideas on to a table.

Objectives

- **Deduce** information about the writer using evidence from the text.
- Think about the reading strategies I use to find and evaluate information from the text.

Reading strategy

- **Deduce**

  Can you be a 'detective' and use evidence in the text to work out hidden meanings? Can you look behind what the writer is saying and work out why it is being said? Look at the things the author chooses to write about. Try to work out what it says about him as a person.

Your task

1 Close-read the paragraphs you have been allocated, paying attention to the information that the writer has given. Highlight the bits of information which you think could tell you something about the author as a person.

2 Discuss the evidence you have selected with a partner and decide what the inclusion of this information tells you about the writer.

For example: In the text the writer says *'I learned to recognise the news addicts and the insomniacs'. This shows us that he is observant. He distinguishes differences between his customers.*

You should present this information in a two-column table as shown on page 65 of the Pupils' Book.

3 Remember you will be asked to share your deductions in the plenary. Using the information from the right-hand column of the table write a brief description of William Woodruff, the writer of the text. Compare your description of William Woodruff with your partner's. What are the similarities and differences between these?

A passion for print

While we were living at Livingstone Road [1]I really began to earn my keep. [2]I took pride in doing so. I started delivering morning and evening newspapers for George and Madge Latham, a young, childless couple in their thirties, who ran a sweets, tobacco and newspaper business on Revidge Road. [3]The Lathams were an honest, hard-working couple. They were Lancashire folk: [4]active, tough, resourceful. They were always cheerful. I was a year below the minimum age, but they took me on just the same; [5]no one enforced the law. They paid me the princely sum of [6]two shillings and sixpence per week, of which I kept a dodger. Mother took the rest. [7]That was my contribution to help pay for the house.

[8]I came to spend so much time with the Lathams that home and school fell into the background. Winter and summer, wet or fine, [9]I got myself up at five to meet George at the newspaper depot in the centre of town about a mile and a half away. I had to run through the dark, hushed streets for half an hour or so. [10]I'd find him waiting for me with his bicycle. On cold mornings his teeth were chattering. Together, we then fought our way in and out of an ill-lit warehouse that served as the newspaper depot. [11]It was a daily hand-to-hand battle with other men to get our newspapers[12]. It was bedlam there.

Once we'd got the [13]warm, damp bundles under our arms, we loaded them and George's bike onto the first tram to Revidge Road at six o'clock. Kneeling on the ribbed floor, we sorted the papers as the tram lurched along. When the floor was wet with melted snow off people's clogs, we used the seats. At Revidge Road, George helped me off the tram. [14]With a bag of newspapers on either shoulder, I began my round. Depending on the weather, I'd be running through the streets for the next hour, or hour and a half. [15]I found it wonderful to have the world to myself.

I had no difficulty knowing which paper went where. [16]Labour people took the [17]*Herald* or *News Chronicle*, Conservatives the *Mail* or the *Telegraph*, Liberals the *Guardian*, the toffs took *The Times*. A switch in newspaper usually meant a switch in political allegiance. [18]I knew how my customers would vote.

Delivering newspapers taught me a lot about human nature. [19]I learned to recognise the news addicts and the insomniacs. In summer, these chaps paced up and down their lawns awaiting my arrival. The way they snatched the paper out of my hand, [20]made me feel important. I knew by the way they rushed to the financial pages that, like most of the rich, they were fearful of losing their money. I'd nothing to lose so the financial crashes left me unmoved. [21]I decided it must be worrying to be rich.

In bad weather, the [22]kind-hearted awaited my arrival with a cup of tea and a bun. The [23]not so kind angrily waved the paper in my face as if I were responsible for the success of Labour at the polls, or the assassination of the head of a foreign state. I felt like saying: 'Look, Mister, I don't write these papers, I just deliver them.' [24]Usually, I kept my mouth shut. [25]One thing I did learn was never to give a man the wrong paper. You've no idea how touchy some people can be. They'd bawl me out as if I'd permanently committed them to the wrong religion.

1 First person recount establishes this as an autobiographical text.
2 Work is clearly important to him.
3 Descriptions of worthy qualities.
4 Further positive adjectives. This suggests he admires these qualities.
5 Acceptance that rules could be changed if it was considered necessary.
6 12.5p equivalent.
7 Shows a responsible attitude.
8 The job grew in importance to him.
9 Evidence of his commitment to the job.
10 The writer can be relied on to turn up.
11 The writer is like 'other men', not a boy.
12 Links with 'Together' at start of previous sentence. A sense of comradeship.
13 Noun phrases add to description. All are positive despite the cold and wet conditions.
14 Heavy work; no bike!
15 Really enjoys it.
16 Learns how to judge people from the newspapers they read.
17 These newspapers no longer exist.
18 Recognises their political leanings.
19 He is observant. He distinguishes the differences between his customers.
20 The job boosts his sense of self worth.
21 He doesn't judge but feels sorry for them.
22 Contrast to the 'news addicts and insomniacs'.
23 Further contrast.
24 He takes the good with the bad without comment.
25 Learns a fundamental rule about newspaper delivery.

The world of work: Annotated text

In time I came to have a [26] large family of newspaper readers. I knew them more closely than they realised. I knew them by the way their houses stared, sat and slept. I closely followed my customers' births, weddings, divorces and deaths. I knew who had gone broke, and who was doing very nicely. I knew when a move was under way. I delivered Dr Michael's paper. He was the great ear, nose and throat specialist who was unable to save his own daughter from a fatal ear infection. '[27] And how is the Michael child?' some customers asked me as if I were a consulting physician.

[28] With a passion for the printed word, I not only delivered newspapers, I read them too. [29] I started every day eager to see what the world was up to.

[30] One thing I did learn, was the way newspapers contradicted each other – that truth is not as straight-forward as I thought it was. [31] A disaster in politics in one paper was a victory in another. I asked myself how could that be? [32] I also learned to be suspicious of the writers who had a simple answer for everything. Every day I read the column by Hannan Swaffer in the *Daily Herald*. Why, if they'd have put Mr Swaffer in charge, the country and the world would have been on its feet again in seven days. [33] I found it confusing.

[34] I asked George Latham what he made of it; after all, he had newsprint all over his hands as I did, and he was much older.

'I'd never deliver the news, Billy, if I tried to make head or tail of it,' he answered. '[35] We're businessmen, Billy. We have our work cut out delivering papers without worrying about what it all means'[36]

From *The Road to Nab End* by William Woodruff

26 Sees his customers almost as family – supported by details of his close observations as a 'people-watcher'.

27 People recognise him as a store of local information.

28 Loves reading. This starts a section on how reading newspapers educated, informed and entertained him.

29 Remember, this was before TV news.

30 He learns about the media's ability to distort the facts.

31 Sees that there are different perspectives and opinions about events.

32 Growing scepticism. Realises life is complicated.

33 Short simple sentence for emphasis.

34 Recognises his employer's wisdom and experience.

35 Includes the writer.

36 The quotation is like 'the last word' – an opinion from someone he respects.

Discoveries

Introduction

These three texts explore what it means to discover something. The texts show the joy of such discoveries through their use of language.

 My first oyster  Educating Rita  The colour of radium

Reading strategies

- hear a reading voice
- infer
- ask questions
- deduce
- feel

Assessment focuses and framework objectives

Select the appropriate objectives for your class from the lists below, grouped by assessment focus. Consider not just their year group but also their starting point for this aspect of reading and the desired focus for the teaching.

Assessment focus 3 – deduce, infer or interpret information, events or ideas from texts

Year 7	Year 8	Year 9
• **R8 Infer and deduce** • R18 Response to a play	• R7 Implied and explicit meanings	• **W7 Layers of meaning**

Assessment focus 5 – explain and comment on writers' uses of language, including grammatical and literary features at word and sentence level

Year 7	Year 8	Year 9
• **R12 Character, setting and mood** • R14 Language choices	• W11 Figurative vocabulary • W12 Formality and word choice • R7 Implied and explicit meanings	• **R7 Compare texts** • **R12 Rhetorical devices** • R14 Analyse scenes

Assessment focus 6 – identify and comment on writers' purposes and viewpoints and the overall effect of the text on the reader

Year 7	Year 8	Year 9
• R9 Distinguish writer's views • R16 Author attitudes	• **R5 Trace developments** • R11 Compare treatments of same theme	• R6 Authorial perspective • R11 Author's standpoint

Discoveries: Sample lesson plan

Educating Rita

Questions 1–2: page 72 of the Pupils' Book

Assessment focus 5 – explain and comment on writers' uses of language, including grammatical and literary features at word and sentence level

Year 7	Year 8	Year 9
• **R12 Character, setting and mood** • R14 Language choices	• W12 Formality and word choice	• R12 Rhetorical devices • R14 Analyse scenes

10 Starter

1. Ask the pupils to read the play extract from the beginning to '*Frank I'm honoured that you chose me.*'
2. Draw attention to the stage directions. Discuss with pupils the way these directions set the scene and present the characters. Make the point that the language draws a contrast between the way Frank and Rita are presented. (See the annotated text on page 55.)

15 Introduction

1. Using an OHT of this section of the text, do a shared reading with the pupils. Focus on the contrast between the language of the two characters. Make the point that Frank speaks in more formal English eg '*I'm honoured that you chose me*' whereas Rita speaks informally and uses slang, non-standard grammar eg *'it's me dinner hour, but listen, I've gorra tell someone.'*
2. Working in pairs, ask pupils to scan the text and identify what Rita found so *'fantastic'* about the production of *Macbeth* she has just seen. Ask them to discuss the way she speaks and the language she uses.
3. Take feedback and annotate on the OHT. Draw out from the discussion the key points: use of questions, colloquial language, repetition, informal register etc. Ask the pupils to consider how this portrayal and the contrast with Frank make the text funny.

Development

1. Working in pairs, ask pupils to read aloud the rest of the extract and discuss how the writer uses the language to make it amusing for the audience.
2. Ask pupils to find three exchanges between Frank and Rita which are intended to be humorous and prepare to feedback in the plenary about why the audience would find them funny.
3. Guided group: work with a group of pupils needing further support.

Plenary

1. Ask pupil pairs to read aloud one of their selected exchanges and explain why the audience would find it funny.
2. Encourage the rest of the class to listen carefully and then comment on how the writer has used the contrast of the language between the two characters to show the humour of the discussion about tragedy.
3. A further lesson could be spent developing the understanding of the characters and the language through question 3 (page 72 of the Pupils' Book) where pupils produce spider diagrams on each character.

Educating Rita

Question 2: page 72 of the Pupils' Book

Assessment focus 5 – explain and comment on writers' uses of language, including grammatical and literary features at word and sentence level

Year 7	Year 8	Year 9
• **R12 Character, setting and mood** • R14 Language choices	• W12 Formality and word choice	• R12 Rhetorical devices • R14 Analyse scenes

Guided session

Introduction to the text	• Recap understanding of the first part of the extract. Explain that in the rest of the extract Frank tries to explain to Rita the difference between 'tragedy' and 'tragic'. Emphasise that the focus of the session will be on how the writer uses language to make Frank and Rita's discussion amusing. Make sure pupils understand the word 'tragedy' before moving on to the strategy check.
Strategy check	• Ask pupils to remember and explain the following reading strategies: **Hear a reading voice** (Ask pupils to think about the voices of the two characters and how these change through the text. Imagine it being spoken on the radio or in a live performance.) **Ask questions** (Why do the characters respond to each other in the way they do? What can you tell about the characters from what they say?) • Remind pupils that the purpose of this guided session is to identify the language which makes this extract amusing.
Independent reading and related task	• Working in pairs ask pupils to read aloud from '*Well, I better get back...*' to the end of the text. As pupils read aloud support those who are hesitant in their reading. • Ask the pupils which bits of the text they found most funny and pick out three quotations as evidence. • Support pupils by modelling one example for them on the OHT (see the annotated text on page 55).
Return to the text: developing response	• Share as a group the quotations chosen by the pupils and mark these on the OHT of the extract. Ask them to explain how the language the characters use and the way they speak make it funny for the audience. Make links with the way the characters speak earlier in the text and any changes you have noticed.
Review	• Invite the group to feedback one example during the plenary and rehearse their reading aloud and explanation. Review the reading strategies used and set personal targets.

Discoveries: Group worksheet

Educating Rita

Question 2: page 72 of the Pupils' Book

Context

As a whole group we have:

- Used the reading strategies: **hear a reading voice**, **ask questions** and **infer**.
- Noted the difference in formality between the language used by the characters Frank and Rita.

Objectives

- Identify how the writer's use of language adds humour to the scene.
- Think about how the staging of a scene can affect the audience's reaction.

Reading strategies

- **Hear a reading voice**
  Think about how the central characters sound and the noises of all the action. What can you hear while you read?
- **Ask questions**
  Ask yourself why the author has written the text in this way. What is the significance of the details the author includes?
- **Infer**
  Can you interpret what the characters say in more than one way?

Your task

1. Work in a group of four. In your group, one pair reads aloud the rest of the text from '*Rita Well, I better get back*' to the end. The other pair should listen carefully and make notes of the parts of the reading that they found most amusing. When the reading is completed, discuss which sections the listeners found amusing.
2. Working in pairs, look closely at the sections you discussed. Pick out three quotations from the text which you found funny. With your partner, discuss why you found this quotation amusing. Pay attention to the more formal English used by Frank and the more colloquial way Rita speaks.
   For example, it is amusing when Rita says if she doesn't get back to her customer's perm it will be a 'tragedy with blood an' guts everywhere' as she is using the imagery of murder and bloodshed from the play Macbeth *to refer to somebody's haircut.*
3. For each quotation you select, write brief notes to explain how the language and the way the characters speak make your chosen quotations funny. Practise reading aloud one or two of them in your pair and ask your partner to point out any parts of your explanation that could be made clearer. You should be prepared to feedback in the plenary.

Educating Rita

Rita [1]*bursts through the door out of breath*

Frank What are you doing here? *(He looks at his watch)* It's Thursday, you ...

Rita *(moving over to the desk, quickly)* I know I shouldn't be here, [2]it's me dinner hour, but listen, I've gorra tell someone, have y' got a few minutes, can y' spare ...?

Frank *([3]alarmed) My* God, what is it?

Rita I had to come an' tell y', Frank, last night, I [4]went to the theatre! A [5]proper one, a professional theatre.

Frank *(sighing)* For God's sake, you had me worried, I thought it was something serious.

Rita No, listen, it was. I went out an' got me ticket, it was Shakespeare, [6]I thought it was gonna be dead borin' ...

Frank Then why did you go in the first place?

Rita I wanted to find out. But listen, it [7]wasn't borin', it was bleedin' great, honest, ogh, it done me in, it was fantastic. I'm gonna do an [8]essay on it.

Frank *(smiling)* Come on, which one was it?

Rita *moves* [9]UP RIGHT CENTRE

Rita '... Out; out, brief candle!
Life's but a walking shadow, a poor player
That struts and frets his hour upon the stage
And then is heard no more. It is a tale
Told by an idiot, full of sound and fury
Signifying nothing.'

[10]**Frank** (*deliberately*) Ah, *Romeo and Juliet.*

Rita (*moving towards* Frank) Tch. Frank! Be serious. I learnt that today from the book. *(She produces a copy of 'Macbeth')* [11]Look, I went out an' bought the book. Isn't it great? What I couldn't get over is how [12]excitin' it was.

Frank *puts his feet up on the desk*

Rita [13]Wasn't his wife a cow, eh? An' that fantastic bit where he meets Macduff an' he thinks he's all invincible. I was on the edge of me seat at that bit. I wanted to shout out an' tell Macbeth, warn him.

Frank You didn't, did you?

Rita Nah. Y' can't do that in a theatre, can y'? It was dead good. It was like a thriller.

Frank Yes. You'll have to go and see more.

Rita I'm goin' to. [14]Macbeth's a tragedy, isn't it?[15]

Frank *nods*

Rita Right.

Rita *smiles at* Frank *and he smiles back at her* [16]Well I just – I just had to tell someone who'd understand.

Frank [17]I'm honoured that you chose me.

Rita *(moving towards the door)* Well, I better get back. I've left a customer with a perm lotion. [18]If I don't get a move on there'll be another tragedy.

Frank No. There won't be a tragedy.

1 Powerful verb introduces Rita's character and contrasts with Frank's calm demeanour.

2 Non-standard grammar – 'me' and colloquial 'gorra' etc establish that Rita is from a different social class and has a regional accent.

3 Not Rita's usual time. Frank is concerned that something is wrong – they know one another already.

4 Exclamation emphasises how important this is – the first time ever.

5 Repetition for emphasis.

6 This shows that Rita is not an academic and not used to live theatre.

7 Repetition of 'it' indicates Rita's excitement by what she has seen – she also speaks rapidly, adding to her sense of awe.

8 She makes the link with her academic aspirations – her character is developing.

9 Stage direction emphasises the dramatic way Rita moves as she prepares to deliver the speech.

10 Ironic. Humour underlines the easy relationship between the two characters.

11 This is a significant act for Rita.

12 Rita displays a good understanding of the play but her language is colloquial and probably the way she speaks normally.

13 Key points she learns about Macbeth.

14 Key point she learns about the play.

15 She confirms her impression – it is an achievement for Rita.

16 Frank is the only one who she could share this with. The stage directions confirm the warmth of their relationship.

17 Frank understands what this means to Rita and is almost humbled by her outburst.

18 Underlines Rita's natural Liverpool street humour.

Rita [18]There will, y'know. I know this woman; she's dead fussy. If her perm doesn't come out right there'll be blood an' guts everywhere.

Frank Which might be quite tragic –

[19]*He throws her the apple from his desk which she catches*

– but it won't be a tragedy.

Rita What?

Frank Well – erm – look; the tragedy of the drama has nothing to do with the sort of tragic event you're talking about. [20]Macbeth is flawed by his ambition – yes?

Rita *(going and sitting in the chair by the desk)* Yeh. Go on.

(She starts to eat the apple)

Frank Erm – it's that flaw which forces him to take the inevitable steps towards his own doom. You see?

Rita *offers him the can of soft drink.* [21]*He takes it and looks at it*

Frank *(putting the can down on the desk)* No thanks. Whereas, Rita, a woman's hair being reduced to an inch of stubble, or – or the sort of thing you read in the paper that's reported as being tragic, 'Man Killed By Falling Tree', is not a tragedy.

Rita It is for the poor sod under the tree.

Frank Yes, it's tragic, absolutely tragic. But it's not a tragedy in the way that *Macbeth* is a tragedy. Tragedy in dramatic terms is inevitable, pre-ordained. Look, now, even without ever having heard the story of *Macbeth* you wanted to shout out, to warn him and prevent him going on, didn't you? But you wouldn't have been able to stop him would you?

Rita No.

Frank Why?

Rita [22]They would have thrown me out the theatre.

Frank [23]But what I mean is that your warning would have been ignored. He's warned in the play. But he can't go back. He still treads the path to doom. But the poor old fellow under the tree hasn't arrived there by following any inevitable steps has he?

Rita No.

Frank There's no particular flaw in his character that has dictated his end. If he'd been warned of the consequences of standing beneath that particular tree he wouldn't have done it, would he? Understand.

[24]**Rita** So – so Macbeth brings it on himself?

Frank Yes. You see he goes blindly on and on and with every step he's spinning one more piece of thread which will eventually make up the network of his own tragedy. Do you see?

[25]**Rita** I think so. I'm not used to thinkin' like this.

Frank It's quite easy, Rita.

Rita It is for you. I just thought it was a dead excitin' story. But the way you tell it you make me see all sorts of things in it. *(After a pause)* [26]It's fun, tragedy, isn't it?

From *Educating Rita* by Willy Russell

19 Writer punctuates Frank's statement with the apple – to distract Rita from going and to focus her attention.

20 Frank treats Rita as an equal – with respect.

21 Frank is absorbed in his explanation.

22 Rita's natural reaction – humour – underlines the contrast between them – she brings something fresh and natural to these sessions.

23 Frank poses a series of questions to make Rita understand.

24 The moment of revelation.

25 Underlines the shift in thinking for Rita and her background.

26 Irony here – Rita is stimulated by the thinking and learning process she is experiencing.

8 Rituals

Introduction

These three texts consider the role of rituals in our cultures. They explore issues such as teenage rites of passage, arranged marriage and religion.

The walk of death

Preparations for marriage

How do Buddhists worship?

Reading strategies

- relate to your own experience
- speculate
- predict what will happen
- empathise
- ask questions
- infer

Assessment focuses and framework objectives

Select the appropriate objectives for your class from the lists below, grouped by assessment focus. Consider not just their year group but also their starting point for this aspect of reading and the desired focus for the teaching.

Assessment focus 2 – understand, describe, select or retrieve information, events or ideas from texts and use quotation and reference to text

Year 7	Year 8	Year 9
• **R2 Extract information** • R4 Note-making	• **R2 Independent research** • R3 Note-making formats	• R1 Information retrieval • R3 Note-making at speed

Assessment focus 3 – deduce, infer or interpret information, events or ideas from texts

Year 7	Year 8	Year 9
• **R8 Infer and deduce**	• R7 Implied and explicit meanings	• **W7 Layers of meaning** • **R7 Compare texts**

Assessment focus 5 – explain and comment on writers' uses of language, including grammatical and literary features at word and sentence level

Year 7	Year 8	Year 9
• **R12 Character setting and mood** • R14 Language choices	• **R10 Development of key ideas**	• **R7 Compare texts**

Rituals: Sample lesson plan

The walk of death

Questions 1–4: page 79 of the Pupils' Book

Assessment focus 3 – deduce, infer or interpret information, events or ideas from texts

Year 7	Year 8	Year 9
R8 Infer and deduce	R7 Implied and explicit meanings	**W7 Layers of meaning**

Assessment focus 5 – explain and comment on writers' uses of language, including grammatical and literary features at word and sentence level

Year 7	Year 8	Year 9
R12 Character, setting and mood R14 Language choices	**R10 Development of key ideas**	**R7 Compare texts**

Starter

1 Using an OHT, reveal the first line of the text to the class. Ask them to work in pairs and to **speculate** on whom the 'Tribe' might be and why they have chosen this name for themselves.

Introduction

1 Using an OHT of the section starting *'It was an ugly old building…'* to *'We're going up the stairs.'* do a shared reading with pupils. Explain to the class that the focus is going to be on character and that you will be contrasting Doc's and Salom's attitude towards Kevin. (See the annotated text on page 61.) Model for pupils how through dialogue and gesture we can **infer** that Doc feels hostile towards Kevin and that Salom is friendlier. Model how you could record this information in a table format. For example, Doc answers Kevin sarcastically. This implies that he is unfriendly towards Kevin. Salom '*slipped an arm around his shoulder*', suggesting that he supports Kevin.

2 Ask pupils to read through the rest of the text. In pairs, one pupil should pick out any words or phrases that reveal Doc's attitude towards Kevin. The other pupil in the pair should pick out evidence of Salom's attitude. The pair should then share their ideas and record them on a table. Ask pupils to **speculate** on why Doc and Salom behave differently.

Development

1 Focusing on the section from *'Going up …'* to the end of the text, ask pupils then to identify how the writer builds up tension in the text. The focus is on the use of language and grammatical features. Ask pupils to work in groups of four. Each pupil should address one of the following areas: evidence of Kevin's growing anxiety, how the others prepare him for the test (what they do and say), how the writer appeals to our senses (comment on the use of a blindfold, what Kevin hears and the description of the building) and Kevin's reaction to the test.

2 Pupils should spend five minutes looking for information and annotating the quotations that they select from the text. They then should share ideas for five minutes. Ask pupils to discuss how they would **feel** in Kevin's position and what they would do.

3 A guided group needing additional support should work on the final paragraphs beginning '*Kevin blinked …*'

Plenary

1 Take feedback by text marking an OHT of the text and annotating. Ask pupils to come to the front to contribute their ideas.

Rituals: Guided reading planner

The walk of death

Questions 3–4: page 79 of the Pupils' Book

Assessment focus 3 – deduce, infer or interpret information, events or ideas from texts

Year 7	Year 8	Year 9
• **R8 Infer and deduce**	• R7 Implied and explicit meanings	• **W7 Layers of meaning**

Assessment focus 5 – explain and comment on writers' uses of language, including grammatical and literary features at word and sentence level

Year 7	Year 8	Year 9
• **R12 Character, setting and mood** • R14 Language choices	• **R10 Development of key ideas**	• **R7 Compare texts**

Guided session

Introduction to the text	• Explain that pupils will be looking at how the writer builds up tension in the final part of the narrative from '*Kevin blinked…*' and that they will explore the use of language and grammatical features. Tell pupils that the focus will include: evidence of Kevin's growing anxiety, how the others prepare him for the test (what they do and say), how the writer appeals to our senses (comment on the removal of the blindfold and the description of the building) and Kevin's reaction to the test. Do a group reading of the rest of the text to the end. Pupils could take the roles of characters and the narrator.
Strategy check	• Explain that pupils will be close reading/exploring the text with a focus in mind and that they will also be asked to **empathise** with the character. Model the reading strategies with the first paragraph of the section, focusing on the use of language and grammatical features. Refer to the annotated text on page 61. Then work with the group on the next paragraph asking questions to draw out meaning.
Independent reading and related task	• In pairs, ask pupils to work on the remaining paragraphs. Remind pupils to pick out evidence of the writer's use of language and grammatical features. Remind them of the focuses: evidence of Kevin's growing anxiety, how the others prepare him for the test (what they do and say), how the writer appeals to our senses (comment on the removal of the blindfold and the description of the building) and Kevin's reaction to the test. Ask pupils to identify one example of each, eg evidence of Kevin's growing anxiety.
Return to the text: developing response	• Ask pupils for their examples and focus on the language used and the grammatical features. In the discussion, draw out how the writer's techniques (language and grammatical features) create tension. Ask pupils to **empathise** with Kevin. How would they feel? What would they do?
Review	• Ask pupils to record key points and prepare to take responsibility for feeding back on this part of the text in the plenary.

The walk of death

Questions 3–4: page 79 of the Pupils' Book

Context

As a whole group we have:

- Explored how dialogue and description reveal character and attitude.
- Contrasted the characters of Doc and Salom.
- Discussed their possible motivation for behaving differently.

Objectives

- Explore how language, sentence structure and punctuation are used to create a sense of tension

Reading strategies

- **Empathise**
  Imagine that you are in the same situation as Kevin. What would you do? Would you do the initiation test or would you refuse and leave? How would you feel – would you be too scared or proud to back out or would you be too frightened to go through with the test?

Your task

1. Spend approximately five minutes close reading the rest of the text. Work in fours. Each person can take the role of a character or narrator.
2. Now focus on the section from *'Going up...'* to the end of the text. Your task is to identify how the writer builds up tension in the text. You will need to focus on the use of language and grammatical features. Look at the use that the writer makes of:
   - adjectives (eg *'faint traffic noises'*, *'breathing hard'*)
   - verbs (eg *'push'*, *'gasped'*)
   - rhetorical questions (eg *'But where was he going?'*, *'How far?'*)
   - variety of sentence structure (eg simple sentences, compound sentences, complex sentences)
3. Work in your groups of four. Each one of you should scan the text for evidence of the following:
   - Kevin's growing anxiety
   - how the others prepare him for the test
   - how the writer appeals to our senses
   - Kevin's reaction to the test.

   Pick out words and phrases and make notes on how language and grammatical features create tension. Share your ideas with the rest of the group. Discuss how you would **feel** in Kevin's position and what you would do.

The walk of death

It was an ugly old building, red brick, with every [1]window smashed and half the inside missing. At night, whenever Kevin would pass those broken windows, they reminded him of [2]sunken skeleton eyes. Now, as they approached it in the twilight, it looked even scarier. He had often imagined how terrifying it would be to be trapped in there in the dark. Now, with a shudder, he had a feeling that was going to be his fate.

'Is that where we're going?' he asked.

[3]Salom grinned. 'That's where we're going.'

Kevin felt his pulse quicken and his heart began to beat faster. He had a notion to run then but, at that moment, [4]Salom slipped an arm around his shoulder, friendly, yet very firm, leading him inside the gaping mouth of that redbrick monster.

'Come, [5]my friend,' he said. 'There's no turning back now.'

It was really [6]dark inside the building, but Kevin wasn't given a chance for his eyes to become accustomed to the blackness. Doc pulled a scarf from his jacket pocket.

'What are you going to do with that?' Kevin asked him.

'Blindfold you,' Doc said [7]stonily.

'What? Are you not going to let me see what I'm doing?'

Maybe they *were* going to make him eat something awful, then guess what it was.

[8]Doc tied the blindfold roughly round his eyes. This boy didn't like Kevin, that was for sure.

'If you're going to tie me up here all night,' Kevin said, trying to sound as if the thought didn't bother him at all, 'someone will have to tell my parents I'm staying over with them.'

Again it was Doc who [9]answered sarcastically. 'You think it's going to be that simple? Stay the night in the old dark warehouse?'

'That's kids' stuff,' Torry said.

'You'll soon know what it is, Kev,' Salom said, at the same time [10]guiding him gently. 'Be careful. We're going up the stairs.'

Going up. That phrase scared him too. Kevin was scared of heights, always had been. [11]He could visualize the stairs in this old building. [12]Broken, crumbling, dangerous. And he was going up them, blindfolded. This had to be the daftest thing he'd ever done.

Step by faltering step he climbed, held gently but firmly by Salom, who [13]encouraged him in his soft voice. 'One more step here, Kev. Now we're turning. Almost there.'

Sometimes a hand would push him roughly forward. He knew who that belonged to – Doc, pushing him so hard he almost tripped.

[14]And he could hear Torry skipping up the stairs behind him, laughing. Looking forward to what was ahead.

[15]What was ahead? How high were they going? It seemed to Kevin that they had been climbing for ever.

He was breathing hard. But it wasn't from the climb. He knew that. It was nerves.

[16]But where was he going?

He could hear faint traffic noises far below.

1 Frightening images.

2 Builds tension.

3 There is a sense that he is enjoying this.

4 Warm, supportive gesture.

5 Friendly attitude.

6 Sensory description increases tension.

7 Evidence of Doc's hostile attitude.

8 'Roughly' suggests Doc's unfriendly attitude.

9 Doc is also unpleasant in the way that he speaks to Kevin.

10 Salom's attitude remains supportive.

11 The fact that Kevin cannot see adds to the tension.

12 Choice of adjectives emphasises the sense of danger that Kevin feels.

13 We get the impression that Salom wants him to succeed.

14 Sounds add to Kevin's unease.

15 Questions show Kevin's anxiety and build tension.

16 Short sentences increase the tension.

Far below.

How far?

He tried to remember how many storeys this warehouse had. Seven? Eight? He'd never counted, in all the times he'd passed here and looked up. Now he wished he had.

They came to a final step and, as Salom turned him on to a landing, Kevin felt a gust of [17] cold night air from a broken window.

17 'Cold' and 'broken' suggest a hostile environment.

'We're here,' Salom said, turning Kevin towards him. 'Doc, take off the blindfold.'

As roughly as he had put it on, Doc [18] whipped it off.

18 A rough gesture.

[19] Kevin blinked. It took a few seconds for his eyes to grow accustomed to the darkness. And it was dark now. No moon. No stars. A cloudy sky overhead.

19 Short sentence leaves the reader also waiting for what Kevin can see.

He looked around him. They were high in the building, not quite on the top floor, but near enough. Dust and broken glass lay everywhere. Behind him, the crumbling stairs he had just climbed. In front of him ...[20]

20 Ellipsis – builds tension. The reader, like Kevin, is unsure of what lies ahead.

Kevin gasped and stepped back. In front of him was nothing. He was standing at the edge of a gaping chasm, a hole that stretched to nothingness below. At the other side of that chasm, it looked a million miles away, was a minute stretch of floor and a smashed window. And all that connected the floor Kevin was standing on to that other side was a narrow wooden beam. Kevin looked at Torry. [21] He was smiling, his hands on his hips. He looked at Doc. There was something malevolent in his eyes. And then he looked at Salom. He stepped on to the beam like an acrobat. Kevin gasped.

21 Contrasts Kevin's fear with the confidence of the others.

[22] Salom grinned. 'You get to the other side, and you are a fully paid-up member of the Tribe.'

22 Like Kevin, the reader does not find out what the challenge is until the very end.

They couldn't be serious. They expected him to cross over there. Below him, a sheer [23] drop? No way!

23 Use of punctuation shows Kevin's fear and shock.

Salom stepped back and gestured to the beam, like a magician. 'Welcome,' he said, 'to the Walk of [24] Death.'

24 The name of the text inspires fear. 'Walk of Death' suggests how dangerous it is.

From *Tribes* by Catherine MacPhail

9 Violent Earth

Introduction

The texts in this unit explore the power of extreme weather conditions and offer pupils the opportunity to explore how language can be used to show the devastating impact of these events.

 Terror in the harbour  The storm  Hurricane

Reading strategies

- rationalise what is happening
- hear a reading voice
- speculate
- see images
- make judgements
- establish a relationship with the writer
- predict what will happen
- read backwards and forwards

Assessment focuses and framework objectives

Select the appropriate objectives for your class from the lists below, grouped by assessment focus. Consider not just their year group but also their starting point for this aspect of reading and the desired focus for the teaching.

Assessment focus 4 – identify and comment on the structure and organisation of texts, including grammatical and presentational features at text level

Year 7	Year 8	Year 9
• R7 Identify main ideas • R15 Endings	• **R10 Development of key ideas**	• **R7 Compare texts**

Assessment focus 5 – explain and comment on writers' use of language, including grammatical and literary features at word and sentence level

Year 7	Year 8	Year 9
• R13 Non-fiction style • R14 Language choices	• W11 Figurative vocabulary • R7 Implied and explicit meanings	• **R7 Compare texts**

Assessment focus 6 – identify and comment on writers' purposes and viewpoints and the overall effect of the text on the reader

Year 7	Year 8	Year 9
• R9 Distinguish writer's views	• R5 Trace developments • R6 Bias and objectivity R11 Compare treatments of same theme	• R6 Authorial perspective • R11 Author's standpoint

Violent Earth: Sample lesson plan

The storm

Question 2: page 92 of the Pupils' Book

Assessment focus 6 – identify and comment on writers' purposes and viewpoints and the overall effect of the text on the reader

Year 7	Year 8	Year 9
• R9 Distinguish writer's views	• **R5 Trace development** • R6 Bias and objectivity • R11 Compare treatments of same theme	• R6 Authorial perspective • R11 Author's standpoint

Starter

1 Explain the meaning of 'alter-ego'. Give an example – Jekyll and Hyde. Explain how the murderous Mr Hyde represented the dark side of Dr Jekyll's character. Ask pupils to think of other examples (eg super-heroes such as Superman, Batman, the Hulk or Spiderman). Working in pairs, ask pupils to discuss the characters and their alter egos and distinguish the differences and tensions created by their alter egos.

2 Then take whole-class feedback, noting any key ideas on the whiteboard.

15 Introduction

1 Using an OHT of the section starting '*I experienced a strange split in my ego*' to '*...the death-stricken faces of these three Sherpas*', do a shared reading with pupils. (See the annotated text on page 67.) Draw out the 'real' Herbert Tichy '*tortured by cold and the fear of death*', ie with instinctive human feelings, and his alter ego who is the critical observer, coolly commenting on events. Make the point that this provides the opportunity for two narrative perspectives, which gives two different viewpoints on events. Ask pupils to **hear a reading voice** and to listen for the change to the alter ego's voice.

Development

1 Ask pupils to close read the rest of the text and to identify the details felt by the instinctive Herbert Tichy and the moment when the critical observer takes over.

Ensure that pupils fully understand these concepts of the 'instinctive character' and the detached 'critical observer'. Encourage pupils to employ the strategy **'rationalise what is happening'** to deepen their understanding of events.

2 Ask pupils to continue the story, in pairs, with one of them preparing the words and thoughts of the instinctive Herbert Tichy, and the other preparing the words and thoughts of his alter ego. This should be prepared as a role play, with notes as prompts, not a script. Stress that it is important that they remain true to the character of Herbert Tichy.

3 Guided group: work with a group of higher-attaining pupils who are less confident with drama activities.

Plenary

1 Select one or two confident pairs to present their role plays and ask pupils to assess the authenticity of the two 'voices' and perspectives. Return to the quotation from the text: '*one part acted instinctively and suffered in the flesh, and the other followed events without feeling or pity, merely as a critical observer.*' Judgements and comments should be based on how closely the role play has adhered to these original words.

2 Read and discuss a short extract from *Dr Jekyll and Mr Hyde* as a development of the theme of the alter ego.

The storm

Question 2: page 92 of the Pupils' Book

Assessment focus 6 – identify and comment on writers' purposes and viewpoints and the overall effect of the text on the reader

Year 7	Year 8	Year 9
• R9 Distinguish writer's views	• **R5 Trace development** • R6 Bias and objectivity • R11 Compare treatments of same theme	• R6 Authorial perspective • R11 Author's standpoint

Guided session

Introduction to the text	• The focus for the group will be to plan the scenario which might follow the ending of the text. You could suggest possible scenarios eg the journey down the mountain or digging into the snow for shelter. Remind pupils that they need to keep in mind the quotation from the text: '*...one part acted instinctively and suffered in the flesh, and the other followed events without feeling or pity, merely as a critical observer.*' Have this quotation enlarged and displayed as a constant reminder. Ask pupils to briefly review what they already know about the writer and his alter ego before preparing their role play.
Strategy check	• Predict what will happen: remind pupils that this involves knowing what has already happened in the text and suggesting what **might happen**, based on the clues they have already picked up.
Independent reading and related task	• Working in pairs, ask pupils to plan their role play with details of the physical conditions being the focus of the instinctive Herbert Tichy and a detached commentary from his alter ego. Suggest they keep returning to the text to see the descriptions of physical conditions and the type of language used by Tichy. They need to make notes as prompts (but **not** write a script).Where extra support is needed, suggest phrases and ideas which might be included in their notes.
Return to the text: developing response	• Ask pupils to present their role plays in this small, safe group. Encourage them to comment on the authenticity of the situation and of the alter ego's response.
Review	• Ask pupils to review the reading strategy used and set a personal target.

The storm

Question 2: page 92 of the Pupils' Book

Context

As a whole group we have:

- Used the reading strategy – hear a reading voice.
- Discussed the meaning of 'alter ego'.

Objectives

- Use note-making skills for a specific purpose.
- Comment on two narrative 'voices' or perspectives in a text.

Reading strategies

- **Hear a reading voice**
  Can you hear the author's voice? Can you hear when it changes to his alter ego's voice?
- **Predict what will happen**
  What do you think will happen next? Remember, your predictions must be based on what you have already read. They must be true to the characters and the situation.

Your task

1 Keep in mind the quotation from the text: '*...one part acted instinctively and suffered in the flesh, and the other followed events without feeling or pity, merely as a critical observer.*' Working in pairs plan the scenario which could follow the ending of the text. This could be the journey down the mountain, digging into the show for shelter or your own idea.

One person will play Herbert Tichy, and focus on describing the physical conditions, and the other person will provide a detached commentary from his alter ego.

Keep returning to the text to see the descriptions of physical conditions and the type of language used by Tichy. Make notes as prompts but do **not write** a script.

2 Practise your role play.

Hint: Try to incorporate quotations from the text into your role play. Think about how your tone of voice and physical actions will help to show the perspective that you are role playing.

3 Share your role play with one other pair and discuss how authentic the role play situations and the two 'voices' are. Discuss changes that could be made to the role play in order to improve it. Decide whether either of the role plays is good enough to present to the class.

The storm

[1, 2, 3]I felt protected and safe in spite of the utter solitude of our bivouac and although I was perhaps sleeping at a point higher and more remote from the world than any other man alive.

I did not dream that night, but waking was a nightmare and I clung to the hope that it was actually a bad dream. The sound of Pasang groaning convinced me that it was real. [4]The side of the tent was being pressed down on my face by some invisible force, preventing me from breathing, and an uproar of rattling, whistling and screaming filled the air. It took me half a minute to realize what had occurred.

[5]The wind had become a hurricane and had torn our tents from their moorings; the tent pegs had snapped. I put out my hand and felt for Pasang, who was groaning, in his sleep perhaps, or perhaps from a presentiment of disaster to come. Stare as I might, no chink of light was to be seen. It was still night.[6]

[7]By the time daylight glimmered through the canvas, the wind had increased in violence. I can't say whether I had slept in the interval or lain awake, but it was now day and I had to come to some decision. I couldn't lie on in a twilight state between sleeping and waking, between life and death; that would be too easy.

The sun penetrated the yellow fabric. It seemed to promise life and warmth, in strange contrast to the [8]icy hurricane which threatened to hurl us down the mountain-side.

I nudged Pasang again.

[9]"Wait? Go down?" he asked.

I didn't know which. I didn't even know whether it was morning or evening, whether we had passed a long day in our wretched tents, or whether the sun had just risen and we still had the day to endure.

"We'll see," I added.

We crept out from under the tent. It was not easy, for the wind kept the canvas tight down on us like a fisherman's net and hugged us.

There was not a cloud in the sky. But we could not always see the sky; it was hidden by thick flurries of snow. [10]A hurricane of a force I had never experienced scourged the snow-covered mountainside. The temperature was thirty to thirty-five degrees below zero. [11]The most horrible part of it was the cloudless blue sky.

I crouched down beside Pasang in the snow. We could not stand up. The wind would have thrown us down or lifted us from the ground.

The other tent was also wrecked. The huddled bodies of Ang Nyima and Adjiba were moulded by the flattened canvas. We gave them a prod. They were still alive and crept out to join us.

The four of us cowered together beside the flattened tents and stared into the vortex. We could only speak in shouts.

[12]"Never known a storm like this," Pasang shouted. "All die."

He repeated it again and again.

[13]I agreed with him. We should all die.

Adjiba and Ang Nyima said nothing. They sat huddled and dumb, their faces a bluish grey, marked by death – no, dead already. Their dark eyes were fixed on mine, asking no questions, hinting no reproach. They were gates to another world, at whose frontier we had now arrived.

1 First person singular establishes this as an autobiographical recount.

2 First sentence sets the scene.

3 Calm start (in contrast to later storm).

4 Slow realisation of where he is and what is happening.

5 First stage of the hurricane.

6 Written in narrative style: past tense; variety of sentence structures; vivid, dramatic descriptions.

7 Intensity of storm increased.

8 With hindsight the writer includes gentle humour.

9 Tichy is the one expected to make the decisions. Direct speech makes it more dramatic.

10 Vivid descriptions.

11 The bright sky is unexpected in hurricane conditions.

12 Direct speech adds to the drama.

13 Short, dramatic simple sentences – appropriate if facing death.

[14]I experienced a strange split in my ego.

Like Pasang and Adjiba and Ang Nyima, [15]I was a poor wretch, tortured by cold and fear of death, whose only comfort in face of the final and utter solitude was derived from the presence of my three companions. [16]And at the same time the other part of me looked down without the least emotion on the four of us. My fate was not at all terrible to this second me. "You've always played fast and loose a bit with this possibility; you can't complain if it has come true. But how can you answer to yourself for the death-stricken faces of these three Sherpas?"[17]

[18]This split personality persisted throughout the events that followed; one part acted instinctively and suffered in the flesh, and the other followed events without feeling or pity, merely as a critical observer, coldly making his own comments upon them.

We were still huddled together, overwhelmed by the violence of nature and incapable of coming to any decision, when [19]suddenly the wind lifted the other tent and threatened to blow it right away. I threw myself on it without thinking and held it down, my body on the tent, my hands in the snow. I had had my mittens stripped off in creeping out of our own tent, but that did not matter very much as I had put my hands in my warm trouser pockets inside an outer windproof smock.

[20]Now they were in contact with the snow, and in the next two or three minutes this is what happened:

The tent was rescued. The Sherpas salvaged it. [21]But I felt a burning sensation in my hands. The pain got worse and throbbed through my whole body.

Probably their warmth melted the snow when they first touched it. The icy hurricane seized on and sucked at the moisture, a hurricane of eighty miles an hour at a temperature of thirty-five degrees below zero.

[21]The pain got worse and worse. I chafed my hands, and beat them against my sides; it did not stop the pain. I thought of creeping into my tent, but it lay like a sail, flat on the snow. [22]I got into a panic, as if I had been on fire – and actually the injuries caused by frost and fire are similar – and started shouting.

The Sherpas, who had been busy so far salvaging the tent, rushed up, and as soon as they realised my disaster, Adjiba hunted under my tent for my mittens.

[23]My watching, critical self showed up again. I saw it all before my eyes as a picture, Pasang and Ang Nyima with their backs pressed against the wind, and myself kneeling crucified between them, my hands outstretched and hidden within the remnants of warmth which might still be my salvation. [24]My animal self relished these few seconds of warmth and shelter.

Adjiba brought my mittens; I seized them. My hands were white and swollen. I felt they were done for, but *we* were not done for yet.

From *Cho Oyu, by favour of the gods* by Herbert Tichy

15 The human part of Tichy experiences the physical suffering.

17 His alter-ego can accept his fate as a predictable consequence of his way of life, but he is conscious of the injustice he has brought on the Sherpas.

19 Increased intensity of the hurricane.

21 His hands are literally burned (frostbitten) by the intense cold.

23 His alter-ego emerges again, observing the scene uncritically.

14 Strangely, Tichy experiences this 'ego-split' at the peak of the hurricane.

16 His alter-ego watches them in a cold, detached manner.

18 The split ego persists.

20 Brief, simple introduction to prepare the reader for a major incident.

22 The instinctive side of Tichy reacts in an understandable way.

24 The 'real' Tichy's experiences.

10 Islands

Introduction

In this unit pupils will explore how texts can be interpreted in different ways and see how a text's purpose influences its form and the language used.

 Cephalonia  Canna  Jamaica

Reading strategies

- relate to previous reading experience
- see images
- infer
- read backward and forwards
- ask questions
- interpret patterns

Assessment focuses and framework objectives

Select the appropriate objectives for your class from the lists below, grouped by assessment focus. Consider not just their year group but also their starting point for this aspect of reading and the desired focus for the teaching.

Assessment focus 2 – understand, describe, select or retrieve information, events or ideas from texts and use quotation and reference to text

Year 7	Year 8	Year 9
R2 Extract information	**R2 Independent research**	R1 Information retrieval
R4 Note-making	R3 Note-making	R3 Note-making at speed
R6 Active reading	R4 Versatile reading	

Assessment focus 4 – identify and comment on the structure and organisation of texts, including grammatical and presentational features at text level

Year 7	Year 8	Year 9
R7 Identify main ideas	**R10 Development of key ideas**	**Sn6 Paragraph organisation**
R13 Non-fiction style		**R7 Compare texts**

Assessment focus 5 – explain and comment on writers' uses of language, including grammatical and literary features at word and sentence level

Year 7	Year 8	Year 9
R13 Non-fiction style	R7 Implied and explicit meanings	**W7 Layers of meaning**
R14 Language choices		**R12 Rhetorical devices**

Islands: Sample lesson plan

Cephalonia

Question 2: page 97 of the Pupils' Book

Assessment focus 5 – explain and comment on writers' uses of language, including grammatical and literary features at word and sentence level

Year 7	Year 8	Year 9
• R13 Non-fiction style • R14 Language choices	• R7 Implied and explicit meanings	• **W7 Layers of meaning**

Starter

1 Briefly consider what language features pupils would expect in writing about a holiday destination (eg lots of excessive descriptions exaggerating the benefits).

2 Ask pupils to work in groups to identify different categories of words in the text: eg adjectives; place names, nouns related to parts of an island. One group could check the meaning of unfamiliar words. Pupils should refer to the context of the passage if they are unsure of a word's class.

3 Groups report to the whole class on the types of words they have found, the quantity of them and what impression they give of the vocabulary of the review. For example, there are fewer adjectives than pupils might expect and they tend not to be excessive descriptions; there are various precise geographical island terms; the inclusion of the quotations from the novel/film along with references to mythology ensures there are some unusual words. Many different places on the island are named.

20 Introduction

1 Remind pupils that they will need to **infer** meanings beyond the literal to appreciate the effects of the language. Focus first on the opening quotation from the text.

a Read the extract aloud and model for pupils how it gives an impression of the island. **Infer** meaning from words like **'half-forgotten'**, **'rises'**, **'inadvisedly'**, and the association with Odysseus.

b Explore the meaning of unfamiliar words to develop this understanding

c Look closely at how the phrasing is made to be almost poetic.

2 Use shared writing to re-write the information as a straightforward factual description and compare that with the original text.

20 Development

1 Pupils close read the remainder of the review, focusing on what they can **infer** from the information given. Key phrases could be given for specific attention if support is needed.

2 Guided reading with a group needing further support with inferring meaning.

Plenary

1 As a class, review the explicit and implied impression the language gives of the island.

2 Discuss what type of reader pupils think the review is written for. Was the review what pupils expected from a description of a holiday destination?

Cephalonia

Question 2: page 97 of the Pupils' Book

Assessment focus 5 – explain and comment on writers' uses of language, including grammatical and literary features at word and sentence level

Year 7	Year 8	Year 9
• R13 Non-fiction style • R14 Language choices	• R7 Implied and explicit meanings	• W7 Layers of meaning

Guided session

Introduction to the text	• Remind pupils that the text uses different types of language to achieve different effects. Parts are formal and factual; other parts contain remarks from the writer and might be more light-hearted. Check which types of words pupils in the group found in the starter and briefly remind them of the class findings.
Strategy check	• **Infer** – as well as understanding the explicit messages of the text, pupils need to infer meanings. This means they will interpret what is being said and look for alternative meanings. It is important to consider what the writer hasn't said as well as the words the writer has chosen. It might help to think about what words and phrases 'suggest' to the reader. • Explore the second paragraph together to check pupils can **infer**. For example, the island is said to be **'beautiful'**. This is an opinion and suggests the writer has visited it. Stating that the island is being filmed might make people think it is worth going to.
Independent reading and related task	• Allocate sections of the text to individuals in the group. If the sections overlap slightly, more than one pupil will have detailed knowledge of that part of the text and this will help generate a discussion. • Pupils close read the text looking for alternative meanings and considering the effect of the particular words chosen. As they work, guide pupils to look at key words and phrases if they need additional support.
Return to the text: developing response	• Review the text, taking feedback from individuals and discussing other meanings suggested by the group. Be explicit about the literal meaning and the inferred interpretation.
Review	• Pupils recall one example of inferring that they have done in the lesson. Discuss how easy or difficult they found it to think of the meanings that were implied, and why. Conclude with why it is useful to be able to **infer** meaning – the reader develops a better understanding of what the writer is saying, questioning and not taking it at face value; it will help when they are writing because they will try to imply rather than state explicit meaning for their reader.

Islands: Group worksheet

Islands

Question 3: page 97 of the Pupils' Book

Context

As a whole group we have:

- Identified the range of words the writer has used in the review.
- Looked closely at the first paragraph to understand the explicit, literal meaning and then consider what other meanings the choice of words suggested or implied to us.

Objectives

- Recognise how writers choose words for deliberate effect.
- Identify layers of implied and explicit meanings.

Reading strategies

- **Infer**
  To infer, you need to read between the lines. This will help you to consider how you, as the reader, are interpreting the meaning. Seeing more than one meaning results in more enjoyment from your reading as you begin to appreciate the writer's craft.

Your task

1 Working individually, close read the remainder of the text. As you read, pause after each sentence to check that you understand the literal meaning and to consider what other meanings might be suggested. Make a note of these.

You could start by commenting on the choice of words in these sentences:

- *'Its capital, Argóstoli, is a* **busy** *town ... with* **bustling** *streets.'*
- *'Because of its size, you* **can't hurry** *a tour of the island, but driving is* **rewarding** *with* **some stunning scenery, especially** *along the coasts.'*
- *'caves which* **drip** *with stalactites'*
- **'Watch your step** *on the* **wet** *footpaths, though!'*
- *'Assos ...* **guards** *a narrow isthmus linked to ...'*

Now look in the text and find some more sentences to **interpret**.

2 When you have finished, work with a partner on one paragraph. Discuss the meanings that you think were implied in that paragraph. Does your partner agree? Did they read it differently and think of any other meanings?

3 Prepare an explanation of one inferred meaning to share with the class in the plenary.

Cephalonia

"The [1]half-forgotten island of Cephalonia [2]rises [3]improvidently and inadvisedly from the Ionian sea; it is an island so immense in antiquity that the very rocks themselves exhale nostalgia and the red earth lies [4]stupefied not only by the sun, but by the impossible weight of memory. The ships of Odysseus were built of [5]Cephalonian pine, his bodyguards were Cephalonian giants, and some maintain that his palace was not in Ithaca but in Cephalonia."

[6]This description of the [7]beautiful Greek island of Cephalonia is taken from the opening pages of Louis de Bernières' best-selling novel, "Captain Corelli's Mandolin". [8]The book is now the subject of a film starring Nicolas Cage, [9]currently being filmed on Cephalonia. Filming is due to finish by the end of August but expect a significant rise in tourist numbers in 2001/02. [10]Beat the rush and go now!

[11]Cephalonia is the largest of the Ionian islands. Its capital, Argóstoli, is a [12]busy town by a bay with a harbour bridge [13]built by the British in the nineteenth century. The town was devastated by the earthquake of 1953 [14](the single most talked about incident in the island's history) and is full of narrow, bustling streets and shops.

[15]Because of its size, you can't hurry a tour of the island, but driving is rewarding with [16]some stunning scenery, especially along the coasts. [17]Lassi and the resorts of the south-west are popular as is Skala to the south-east. Sami on the east coast is a good base and convenient for hydrofoil trips to other islands including neighbouring Ithaca. It's also the [18]site of the Captain Corelli film set.

Within a short drive of Sami are two [19]"must-dos" for any visitor. First, the Dhrogaráti caves which drip with [20]stalactites. The largest is the size of a concert hall and indeed, the acoustics are so good, it is put to that very purpose. [21]Watch your step on the wet footpaths, [22]though! Second is the subterranean cave-lake of Melissáni. [23]Here, part of the limestone roof of a cave collapsed, creating a beautiful place with deep blue water struck by sunlight. [24]According to legend, the nymph Melissáni drowned herself here when she was spurned by Pan.

[25]Arguably Cephalonia's prettiest village is Fiskardo right on the northern tip. Undamaged by the 1953 earthquake, the harbour is surrounded by eighteenth century Venetian houses and is a popular berth for yachts.

[26]Assos is an unspoilt village on the north-west coast. It guards a narrow isthmus linked to a peninsula of steep terraces leading to a ruined Venetian fortress. Just south of [27]Assos is the most beautiful beach on the island and one of the most beautiful in Europe, Myrtos Bay. The subject of countless postcards, the beach at Myrtos is [28]pebbly, but almost white and the sea is "platonic in its presentation of azure and turquoise, emerald, viridian, and lapis lazuli" – [29]Louis de Bernières again.

Cephalonia is one of the [30]most beautiful if not the most beautiful of all the Greek islands. [31]Go now! [32]Oh, and take a copy of "Captain Corelli's Mandolin" with you.

From *www.doyoo.co.uk*, review of holiday destination by 'Picasso'

1 Suggests not over-crowded but also perhaps undervalued.
3 As if it shouldn't really be there.
5 Repetition emphasises its importance.
7 Writer's opinion added.
9 Because website can be updated, current information can be given.
11 Facts given in third paragraph. Reads like a formal opening to an information text.
13 Mentions this to make us feel part of the island?
15 We already know it is the 'largest' Ionian island. Links back to previous paragraph.
17 Points out likely interest in the main towns.
19 Informal language, as if chatting to us. Inverted commas indicate this.
21 Advice given as imperative command.
23 A description we can picture here.
25 'Arguably' introduces it as an opinion.
27 No doubts here!
29 References to *Captain Corelli's Mandolin* are woven throughout the review.
31 Short command said in a light-hearted tone. Encouraging us to go, but not pushing.

2 Makes it sound alive/moving.
4 Motionless, lethargic.
6 Makes link with paragraph 1.
8 Of interest to readers who have seen the film or read the book.
10 Imperative style of advice. Exclamation mark lightens the tone.
12 'Busy' and 'bustling' suggest lively and popular, but also crowded and noisy?
14 Aside (in brackets) adds a personal remark.
16 Another positive adjective, but 'some' implies that not all scenery is 'stunning'.
18 Reminds us about the film.
20 'Drip' is appropriate – literally dripping is causing them to form. Also, implies lots of them.
22 Addition of 'though' makes sentence sound more informal.
24 Text gives a range of information. This links with the reference in *Captain Corelli's Mandolin* to legend of Odysseus.
26 Suggests its geographical position but also suggests protects something valuable.
28 'Pebbly' could be a criticism, but the quotation emphasises the colours but also suggests something valuable, like precious jewels.
30 Repetition of 'most beautiful'.
32 Informal sentence to end paragraph.

11 Aliens and UFOs

Introduction

The three texts in this unit all explore the ideas of worlds beyond our own.

 The War of the Worlds

 Explore the universe/Age of Mythology

 Alien contact

Reading strategies

- infer
- deduce
- speculate
- establish a relationship with the narrator

Assessment focuses and framework objectives

Select the appropriate objectives for your class from the lists below, grouped by assessment focus. Consider not just their year group but also their starting point for this aspect of reading and the desired focus for the teaching.

Assessment focus 3 – deduce, infer or interpret information, events or ideas from texts

Year 7	Year 8	Year 9
• **R8 Infer and deduce**	• R7 Implied and explicit meanings	• **W7 Layers of meaning**

Assessment focus 4 – identify and comment on the structure and organisation of texts, including grammatical and presentational features at text level

Year 7	Year 8	Year 9
• R7 Identify main ideas • R10 Media audiences	• **R10 Development of key ideas**	• **R7 Compare texts**

Assessment focus 5 – explain and comment on writers' uses of language, including grammatical and literary features at word and sentence level

Year 7	Year 8	Year 9
• R14 Language choices	• R7 Implied and explicit meanings • **R10 Development of key ideas**	• **W7 Layers of meaning** • **R12 Rhetorical devices**

Assessment focus 6 – identify and comment on writers' purposes and viewpoints and the overall effect of the text on the reader

Year 7	Year 8	Year 9
• R9 Distinguish writer's views	• **R5 Trace developments** • R11 Compare treatments of same theme	• R11 Author's standpoint

Explore the universe/Age of Mythology

Questions 1–2: page 109 of the Pupils' Book

Assessment focus 4 – identify and comment on the structure and organisation of texts, including grammatical and presentational features at text level

Year 7	Year 8	Year 9
• R7 Identify main ideas • R10 Media audiences	• **R10 Development of key ideas**	• **R7 Compare texts**

Assessment focus 5 – explain and comment on writers' uses of language, including grammatical and literary features at word and sentence level

Year 7	Year 8	Year 9
• R14 Language choices	• R7 Implied and explicit meanings • **R10 Development of key ideas**	• **W7 Layers of meaning** • **R12 Rhetorical devices**

Starter

1 Ask pupils to work in pairs and to skim read each of the advertisements. Ask them to discuss what type of magazine these adverts might be found in and the possible readership of the magazine. Answers might include that these adverts could be placed in a science/astronomy magazine and that a possible audience might be experts or those with an interest in this area.

2 Pose the question: how do the images in each advert convey different perspectives about life beyond Earth? Give pupils two minutes to discuss ideas in pairs. Take feedback, drawing out the use of a scientific image in the first and a mythological image in the second. Contrast how one image reflects a futuristic vision of space and that the other image draws on historical interpretations of life beyond Earth.

Introduction

1 Explain that pupils will be comparing and contrasting the advertisements. Give pupils three minutes in pairs to discuss how they could compare the advertisements. In feedback draw out the use of: titles, layout and organisation of ideas, the type of language used (eg emotive, factual, etc), fonts, images.

2 Use these points to establish a checklist for group and guided work in the development part of the lesson. Making reference to the two texts, model as the first point on the checklist – 'the title'. Draw out the directive language used in both titles to engage the reader. Contrast the factual language of the first with the emotive description of the second.

Development

1 Ask pupils to close read each text. Then ask pupils to work in groups of four. In each group, ask one pair to look at layout and organisation of ideas, and the other pair at language. Ask pupils to refer to the checklist to identify specific features of the text that they will comment on, eg **emotive language**. Make sure that pupils record their ideas, commenting on the text feature and the effect on the reader. Pupils should then reassemble in their group of four and each pair contribute on the use and effect of layout and language conventions.

2 Guided group: work with a group of pupils needing further support. This group will focus on the use of language.

Plenary

1 Take feedback from each group. You could record ideas on an OHT.

Explore the universe/Age of Mythology

Question 2: page 109 of the Pupils' Book

Assessment focus 5 – explain and comment on writers' uses of language, including grammatical and literary features at word and sentence level

Year 7	Year 8	Year 9
• R14 Language choices	• R7 Implied and explicit meanings • **R10 Development of key ideas**	• **W7 Layers of meaning** • **R12 Rhetorical devices**

Guided session

Introduction to the text	• Tell pupils that they are going to focus on the writers' use of language in the two advertisements. Ask pupils what sort of language they would expect to find in a text on space. Draw out the use of factual language and scientific terms. Explain that you will also be looking for examples of emotive language, directive language, powerful adjectives, verbs and adverbs. • Recap with pupils the meaning of these terms and create a checklist on the board or flip chart.
Strategy check	• **Infer** and **deduce** – explain that pupils will be close reading the text with a language focus in mind. Tell them that they will be selecting words and phrases and making notes on the words and phrases that they have selected, explaining their effect on the reader, ie why they have been used. Explore how the strategies will support this.
Independent reading and related task	• Ask pupils to work in groups of three. Ask each group to look at one advertisement. Using the checklist established in the introduction to the lesson, ask pupils to identify and comment on the use of language in the text. Circulate, working with each group to develop discussion and probe ideas.
Return to the text: developing response	• Ask the groups to share their findings. Encourage pupils to use the correct terminology to describe language features and to comment on the effects of the language used. Ensure pupils compare and contrast the use of language in both texts. Pose the question: how is language suited to audience and purpose? Offer support to pupils in reaching a view on this.
Review	• Ask pupils to synthesise ideas and prepare to feedback key points in the plenary.

Aliens and UFOs: Group worksheet

Explore the universe/Age of Mythology

Question 2: page 109 of the Pupils' Book

Context

As a whole group we have:

- Established the purpose and audience of the advertisements.
- Contrasted how they present the same theme in different ways.
- Established a checklist of language and layout conventions to explore when contrasting the texts.
- Contrasted the titles of both advertisements.

Objectives

- Compare how the language used in each advertisement presents a different view of life beyond Earth.
- Comment on how the information in each advertisement is laid out.

Reading strategies

- **Infer**
  Look closely at the language used in each advertisement. Read between the lines. How does the different type of language used in each advertisement suggest a different viewpoint of life beyond Earth?
- **Deduce**
  Be a 'detective'. Look at the fonts and the images used. How do they suggest different interpretations of extra-terrestrial life?

Your task

1. Work in groups of four. Each pair should look at one advertisement.
2. Close read your advertisement. Using the checklist for language you created earlier, pick out examples of the language used.
3. Discuss what you have identified with your partner. Work together to make notes on your advertisement, commenting on:
   - what the language feature is
   - why you have identified the feature
   - its effect on the reader.
4. Share your ideas with the other pair in your group, noting down the points they make.
5. All of you should then discuss the fonts and images used in both advertisements and note down your ideas.

   Hint: Think about the typeface used in the first advertisement which is clear and bold to reflect its scientific angle. Compare this to the gothic typeface of the second to reflect its mythological theme.
6. Prepare to feedback the most interesting points to the rest of the class in the plenary.

1 Factual title. Imperative language. 'Explore' conveys excitement and potential of the unknown.
3 Information is clearly laid out and explained.
5 Factual language describes the technological approaches to the study of life beyond Earth.
7 Suggests the course is exciting and cutting-edge.

[1]Explore the universe[2]
from Jodrell Bank

A programme of part-time courses in astronomy
[3]Life in the Universe and SETI – An introduction to astronomy which focuses on our own cosmic origins and [4]discusses progress in the [5]search for extraterrestrial life.
[6]Introduction to Radio Astronomy – A short course featuring the [4]opportunity to use our radio telescopes either in a weekend visit to Jodrell Bank or over the internet.
Explore the Radio Universe – Our major course on radio astronomy describing its history, techniques and achievements. Students will [4]make their own observations and analyse data from the Jodrell Bank telescopes.
[7]Frontiers of Modern Astronomy – A more advanced course explaining Jodrell research on Stellar Explosions, Pulsars, Gravitational Lenses, the Big Bang and the Cosmic Microwave Background.[8]
Courses consist of 12–24 weeks of part-time home study and lead to the award of Certificates of Credit which can count towards higher awards.
Fees range from £115–£165 for UK/EU students.
Further details and instructions on how to apply are available on our website.
Astronomy Distance Learning, Jodrell Bank Observatory, The University of Manchester, Macclesfield, Cheshire SK11 9DL, United Kingdom.
E-mail: DL-INFO@jb.man.ac.uk
Tel: 01477 572650 Fax: 01477 571618
www.jb.man.ac.uk/distance

From the University of Manchester

2 Bold, clear typeface in original emphasises the scientific slant of the advert.
4 These three phrases imply active participation in the search for extraterrestrial life.
6 Clear and objective language used to describe the possibility of life beyond Earth.
8 Technical terms give a scientific feel to the advertisement.

1 Reference to mythology suggests ancient perspective of life beyond Earth.
3 Directive language. Implies excitement and potential power of the gods.
5 Directive language engages the reader. Suggests that the reader too can be powerful.
7 Active verbs promote sense of excitement.
9 Suggests an existence far away. The language of legends.

[1]Age of Mythology

[2]From the creators of Age of Empires and The Age of Kings
[3]Unleash the [4]wrath of the gods

[5]Enter a world where [6]legends live on and
the will of the gods [5]decides the fate of mortal men.
[7]Build [8]majestic temples, farm the [8]fertile valleys and seek
out [8]wealth in [9]distant realms. [10]Join brave heroes
in the greatest battles of mythology, from the walls of Troy
to the gates of the Underworld. Summon mighty
minotaurs to smash enemy citadels or
call down fire from the skies.
History will never be the same again.
Microsoft game studios
www.agemythology.co.uk

From Microsoft game studios

2 Gothic font in original contributes to mythological theme.
4 Emotive language. Suggests the threatening nature of power.
6 Reinforces the mythological theme.
8 Glorifies the supernatural.
10 Emotive. Glorifies the gods. Gives them admirable qualities, as if they really exist.

12 Food, glorious food

Introduction

The texts in this unit explore the changing views of food.

 The story of Cadbury's chocolate

 Food has four seasons

 Oliver Twist

Reading strategies

- relate to your own experience
- read backwards and forwards
- infer
- deduce
- relate to previous reading experience
- establish a relationship with the writer

Assessment focuses and framework objectives

Select the appropriate objectives for your class from the lists below, grouped by assessment focus. Consider not just the year group but also the starting point for this aspect of reading and the desired teaching focus.

Assessment focus 2 – understand, describe, select or retrieve information, events or ideas from texts and use quotation and reference to text

Year 7	Year 8	Year 9
• **R2 Extract information** • R4 Note-making	• **R2 Independent research** • R3 Note-making formats	• R1 Information retrieval • R3 Note-making at speed

Assessment focus 3 – deduce, infer or interpret information, events or ideas from texts

Year 7	Year 8	Year 9
• **R8 Infer and deduce**	• R7 Implied and explicit meanings	• **W7 Layers of meaning**

Assessment focus 4 – identify and comment on the structure and organisation of texts, including grammatical and presentational features at text level

Year 7	Year 8	Year 9
• R7 Identify main ideas	• **R10 Development of key ideas**	• **W8 Connectives for developing thought** • **R7 Compare texts**

Assessment focus 5 – explain and comment on writers' uses of language, including grammatical and literary features at word and sentence level

Year 7	Year 8	Year 9
• R14 Language choices	• **W11 Figurative vocabulary** • **R10 Development of key ideas**	• **R12 Rhetorical devices**

Food, glorious food: Sample lesson plan

Oliver Twist

Questions 1–2: page 122 of the Pupils' Book

Assessment focus 3 – deduce, infer or interpret information, events or ideas from texts

Year 7	Year 8	Year 9
• **R8 Infer and deduce**	• R7 Implied and explicit meanings	• **W7 Layers of meaning**

10 Starter

1 Using an OHT, show pupils the first two sentences of the text only. Ask them to work in pairs to comment on theme, atmosphere and setting and viewpoint, and how this is suggested through the author's choice of language.

15 Introduction

1 Explain to pupils that Dickens wrote to entertain his audience but also to highlight social concerns of the time. Tell pupils that this extract is concerned with the poor and cruel conditions of orphans in the early nineteenth century and that you will be exploring how the reader can **infer** that Dickens' sympathy lies with the children.

2 Use an OHT of the section starting '*The room in which*' down to '*might have been cast thereon*.' Draw out how the description of the austere environment contributes to the harsh treatment of the boys. Comment on the use of the word *'gruel'* which implies that the food was very unpleasant. Look closely at the boys' behaviour when they have finished their portion and how this emphasises their pitiful and starved condition. (Refer to the annotated text on page 83).

25 Development

1 Ask pupils to close read to the end of the text. Tell them that they should then scan the text looking for further examples that suggest that Dickens' sympathy lies with the orphans. They should look for:

- The way in which Oliver and the other children are described.
- The way that the adults are portrayed.

Encourage pupils to also look for descriptions that suggest the cruel treatment of the orphans. Ask pupils to record their ideas on a point–evidence–explanation table.

2 Guided group: work with a group of higher-attaining pupils to focus on narrative voice and author's intentions.

10 Plenary

1 Ask pupils to share their ideas with another pair and add any points they may not have.

2 Tell pupils that they will be working in their group of four to prepare a two-minute presentation on what the writer is thinking, ie what social comment they think that Dickens is making in this extract. They will need to use evidence from the text to support their points.

3 Groups will then present to the rest of the class.

Oliver Twist

Questions 1–2: page 122 of the Pupils' Book

Assessment focus 3 – deduce, infer or interpret information, events or ideas from texts

Year 7	Year 8	Year 9
• **R8 Infer and deduce**	• R7 Implied and explicit meanings	• **W7 Layers of meaning**

Guided session

Introduction to the text	• Explain to pupils that they will be reading the text to explore the themes of poverty, power and depravity in the text and how these themes and the author's standpoint are conveyed through the descriptions of character, setting and atmosphere. • Check pupil understanding of these themes and terms.
Strategy check	• Explain that they will read the text to **infer** and **deduce** how the themes are represented through the use of language, dialogue and description. Focus pupils on the need to interpret what the different characters say and try to link this to the themes they are exploring. Explain that they need to investigate the text, sometimes filling in gaps to link pieces of evidence together. Prompt pupils to keep their task in mind as they find relevant information.
Independent reading and related task	• Ask pupils to work in groups of three. They should close read the text, then collaborate to scan the text for evidence of how the themes of poverty, power and depravity are represented through the use of language, dialogue and description. (Refer to the annotated text on page 83 to help you with this.) You might wish to ask each group to focus on one theme in particular when reading the text.
Return to the text: developing response	• Ask pupils to share and discuss ideas as a whole group. They should focus on the use of language and author's standpoint. (If pupils need support with this, use the annotated text to help you to model the reading strategies they should apply to help them with this task.)
Review	• Ask pupils to return to their groups of three. Each group will script a two-minute presentation to give to the rest of the class during the plenary. The presentations will be in role. One group will assume the voice of the author and one will adopt the voice of an orphan in the text. Drawing on evidence from the text, each group will devise a short speech which highlights the plight of orphans in Dickens' time. Encourage pupils to draw in the themes they have discussed and refer to evidence from the text in role, as appropriate.

Food, glorious food: Group worksheet

Oliver Twist

Questions 1–2: page 122 of the Pupils' Book

Context

As a whole group we have:

- Discussed Dickens' viewpoint and purpose for writing.
- Established that his sympathy lies with the children.
- Explored how we can deduce that Dickens' sympathy lies with the children through the descriptions of the setting and characters.

Objectives

- Look for evidence from the text that shows the writer's views of the orphaned children.

Reading strategies

- **Deduce**
  Be a 'detective'. Look closely at the language used in the text.
- **Infer**
  Read between the lines. What does the type of language used in the text suggest about Charles Dickens' view of the treatment of orphaned children?

Your task

1 Close read to the end of the text.

2 Work in pairs to scan the text, looking for further examples that suggest that Dickens' sympathy lies with the orphans. You should look for:

- The way in which Oliver and the other children are described. (How do they look? How do they act?)
- The way that the adults are portrayed. (Are there differences between the description of the adults and the children?)
- The environment of the school. (How is the hall described?)

You should also look for any descriptions that suggest the cruel treatment of the orphans. (Think about how the adults treat the children. Pick out any powerful words and phrases that suggest cruelty.) Record your ideas in a 3-point list. An example has been provided for you:

Point – Dickens highlights the lack of food.

Evidence – He describes the boys as *'sucking their fingers most assiduously'*.

Explanation – This suggests that the boys are so desperately hungry that they are making sure that they have eaten every last bit of the gruel.

3 Prepare to discuss your notes with another pair in the plenary.

Food, glorious food: Annotated text

Oliver Twist

The room in which the boys were fed, was [1]a large stone hall, with a copper at one end: out of which [2]the master, dressed in an apron for the purpose, and assisted by one or two women, ladled the [3]gruel at meal-times. Of this [4]festive composition each boy had one porringer, [5]and no more – except on occasions of great public rejoicing, [6]when he had two ounces and a quarter of bread besides. The bowls [7]never wanted washing. [8]The boys polished them with their spoons till they shone again; and when they had performed this operation (which never took very long, the spoons being nearly as large as the bowls), they would sit staring at the copper, with such eager eyes, as if they could have [9]devoured the very bricks of which it was composed; employing themselves, meanwhile, in sucking their fingers most assiduously, with the view of catching up any stray splashes of gruel that might have been cast thereon. [10]Boys have generally excellent appetites. Oliver Twist and his companions [11]suffered the [12]tortures of slow starvation for three months: at last they got so [13]voracious and wild with hunger, that one boy, who was tall for his age, and hadn't been used to that sort of thing (for his father had kept a small cookshop), hinted darkly to his companions, [14]that unless he had another basin of gruel *per diem*, he was afraid he might some night happen to eat the boy who slept next him, who happened to be a weakly youth of tender age. He had a wild, hungry eye; and they implicitly believed him. A council was held; lots were cast who should walk up to the master after supper that evening, and ask for more; and it fell to Oliver Twist.

The evening arrived; the boys took their places. The master, [15]in his cook's uniform, stationed himself at the copper; his pauper assistants ranged themselves behind him; the gruel was served out; and a long grace was said over the short commons. The gruel disappeared; the boys whispered to each other, and winked at Oliver; while his next neighbours nudged him. [16]Child as he was, he was desperate with hunger, and reckless with misery. He rose from the table; and [17]advancing to the master, basin and spoon in hand, said, somewhat alarmed at his own temerity:

'Please, sir, I want some more.'

The master was a [18]fat, healthy man; but he turned very pale. He gazed in stupefied astonishment on the small [19]rebel for some seconds, and then clung for support to the copper. The assistants were paralysed with wonder; the boys with fear.

'What!' said the master at length, in a faint voice.

'Please, sir,' replied Oliver, '[20]I want some more.'

The master [21]aimed a blow at Oliver's head with the ladle; pinioned him in his arms; and shrieked aloud for the beadle.

The board were sitting in solemn conclave, when Mr. Bumble rushed into the room in great excitement, and addressing the gentleman in the high chair, said,

[22]'Mr. Limbkins, I beg your pardon, sir! Oliver Twist has asked for more!'

There was a general start. [23]Horror was depicted on every countenance.

'For [24]*more!*' said Mr. Limbkins. 'Compose yourself, Bumble, and

1 Adjectives emphasise the inhospitable environment.
2 Power relations established.
3 Unappetising description.
4 Ironic.
5 Emphasises the lack of food given to the boys and suggests how strictly this was controlled.
6 Irony.
7 Emphasises the hunger of the boys.
8 Pitiful description – suggests the deprivation of the boys.
9 Social comment – 'devoured' suggests the boys were starving.
10 Dickens' voice – social comment.
11 Explicit authorial stance.
12 Emotive. Extreme description of their condition.
13 Emotive adjectives emphasise the cruelty of their situation.
14 Dickens suggests that extreme conditions can lead to extreme behaviour.
15 Irony? Contrast the situation of the adult against the child.
16 'Desperate' and 'misery' convey author's viewpoint.
17 Suggests Oliver's fear and trepidation.
18 Direct contrast with the children.
19 The master's view, and Dickens' juxtaposition of 'small' and 'rebel' – diminutive yet powerful.
20 Simple statement loaded with pathos.
21 The violence of their situation.
22 Exclamation shows their surprise and indignation.
23 Exaggerated reaction.
24 Exclamation.

answer me distinctly. Do I understand that he asked for more, after he had eaten the supper allotted by the dietary?'

'He did, sir,' replied Bumble.

'That boy will be hung,' said the gentleman in the white waistcoat. 'I know that boy will be hung.'

Oliver was ordered into instant confinement; and a bill was next morning pasted on the outside gate, offering a reward of five pounds to anybody who would take Oliver Twist off the hands of the parish.

From *Oliver Twist* by Charles Dickens

13 New worlds

Introduction

The three texts in this unit explore some of the exciting discoveries which encourage exploration beyond our everyday lives and take us into previously unknown realms.

In search of the true explorer

Up the Amazon

Jim, our scans now show...

Reading strategies

- see images
- rationalise what is happening
- interpret patterns
- infer
- read backwards and forwards

Assessment focuses and framework objectives

Select the appropriate objectives for your class from the lists below, grouped by assessment focus. Consider not just their year group but also their starting point for this aspect of reading and the desired focus for the teaching.

Assessment focus 3 – deduce, infer or interpret information, events or ideas from texts

Year 7	Year 8	Year 9
• **R8 Infer and deduce** • R9 Distinguish writer's views	• R7 Implied and explicit meanings • R8 Transposition	• **W7 Layers of meaning**

Assessment focus 4 – identify and comment on the structure and organisation of texts, including grammatical and presentational features at text level

Year 7	Year 8	Year 9
• R7 Identify main ideas	• **R5 Trace developments** • **R10 Development of key ideas**	• **R7 Compare texts**

Assessment focus 6 – identify and comment on writers' purposes and viewpoints and the overall effect of the text on the reader

Year 7	Year 8	Year 9
• R9 Distinguish writer's views • R16 Author attitudes	• R6 Bias and objectivity • R11 Compare treatments of same theme	• R11 Author's standpoint

In search of the true explorer

Questions 1–2: page 126 of the Pupils' Book

Assessment focus 6 – identify and comment on writers' purposes and viewpoints and the overall effect of the text on the reader

Year 7	Year 8	Year 9
• R9 Distinguish writer's views	• R6 Bias and objectivity • R11 Compare treatments of same theme	• R11 Author's standpoint

10 Starter

1 Refer pupils to the photograph of the explorer on page 125 of the Pupils' Book. Ask them to discuss the character in the picture in pairs and comment on his posture, clothes and way he is presented. Give them a few minutes and then take feedback of their main impressions. Establish that this is someone from a different period of time, who might have been an explorer. Link to any prior knowledge pupils might have about explorers.

2 In pairs, ask pupils to write a definition of an explorer which they will return to in the plenary.

20 Introduction

1 Using an OHT of the first five paragraphs of the extract do a shared reading with pupils. (See the annotated text on page 89.) Ask pupils to consider the title of the extract. What does the use of the word 'true' suggest about the writer's attitude? Compare the first paragraph with the picture used in the starter activity. Note how the writer involves the reader from the outset and uses the language to present this image of an explorer as a 'caricature'. Work through the text sharing and annotating to identify the image the writer expects the reader to have of an explorer.

2 Working in pairs, ask pupils to pick out the reasons the writer gives for why this image of an explorer is out-of-date. Take feedback and mark these on the OHT. Note the contrast drawn between modern explorers and Victorian explorers and their different views on the nature of exploration.

20 Development

1 Working in pairs, ask pupils to close read the rest of the extract to identify the key features of an explorer from the opinions the writer sought and how these contribute to his own views expressed at the end of the extract.

2 Pupils write a definition of an explorer that they think the writer would agree with and compare this with the ones they wrote at the beginning of the lesson.

3 Guided group: work with a group of pupils needing further support with this text.

10 Plenary

1 Select pupil pairs to feedback their new definitions of an explorer and say why they think the writer would agree with them.

2 As definitions are presented, ask the rest of the class to listen carefully and comment on how well the definitions fit the views expressed by the writer in the extract.

3 Draw together the discussion by reminding the pupils of the objective, which was to identify the writer's views in this extract.

4 Homework could be to compare the 'Profile of an Explorer' which they did in the pre-reading tasks with the views expressed in the extract and produce a new version.

In search of the true explorer

Question 2: page 126 of the Pupils' Book

Assessment focus 6 – identify and comment on writers' purposes and viewpoints and the overall effect of the text on the reader

Year 7	Year 8	Year 9
• R9 Distinguish writer's views	• R6 Bias and objectivity • R11 Compare treatments of same theme	• R11 Author's standpoint

Guided session

Introduction to the text	• Re-cap understanding of the writer's view of explorers as presented in the first part of the extract. Explain that in the rest of the extract the writer uses facts and opinions from a number of modern explorers in order to arrive at his own definition of an explorer. • Read the rest of the extract with the group and model for them picking out the opinions on a pupil whiteboard.
Strategy check	• Ask pupils to remember and explain the following reading strategies: **a** reading backwards and forwards **b** ask questions of the text. • Remind pupils that the purpose of this guided session is to identify the writer's views. Explain that **reading backwards and forwards** will help them to build up their understanding of the writer's views, some of which are initially difficult to understand. • Remind pupils that the **questions they ask** of the text should all be aimed at developing their understanding of the writer's view of the topic.
Independent reading and related task	• Ask pupils to skim read the last four paragraphs and select any other evidence which the writer gives to widen the definition of an explorer. **eg** *'Astronomers are using larger and more sensitive telescopes to examine the farthest reaches of the cosmos'.* • Support pupils by working through the first paragraph and then individually as they work independently.
Return to the text: developing response	• Ask pupils to share the evidence they have selected. Ask them to explain how this additional evidence helps us to understand the definition of an explorer which the writer presents. • As a group, write a definition of an explorer which the writer would agree with and model this for the pupils. Compare this with the definitions they wrote in the starter.
Review	• Invite the group to feedback during the plenary by rehearsing their definitions and why they think the writer would agree with them. Review the reading strategies used and set personal targets.

New worlds: Group worksheet

In search of the true explorer

Question 2: page 126 of the Pupils' Book

Context

As a whole group we have:

- Used the reading strategies: **read backwards and forwards** and **ask questions**.
- Noted the contrast drawn by the writer between explorers of the past and the present.

Objectives

- Recognise bias (opinion) and objectivity (fact) in a text.
- Comment on the writer's views given in a text.

Reading strategies

- **Read backwards and forwards**
  Clarify your understanding by making links back to what you have just read and forward to what is coming next. You should use this strategy to build up your understanding of the writer's views.
- **Ask questions**
  Ask questions all the time. Why has the author written the text in this way? What is the significance of the details the author includes? Do the details mean something?

Your task

1. Skim read the rest of the text quickly to get an idea of the main facts and opinions which the writer uses in order to arrive at his own definition of an explorer. Pick out any opinions or facts which the writer gives to define an explorer. For example, the views from explorers like Sir Ranulph Fiennes: *An explorer is 'someone who has done something that no human has done before and also done something scientifically useful'.*
2. Share your findings with your partner and discuss what they tell you about the writer's view of an explorer. Review the evidence you have found in the text and write your own definition of an explorer which you think the writer would agree with based on this evidence. Make sure you use your own words and do not repeat any of the definitions from the text.
3. Compare this definition with the one you wrote at the beginning of the lesson. Make a list of the similarities and differences between the two definitions. Are there any changes you would make to your first definition now that you have read the text? What would these be?
4. Rewrite your own definition of an explorer and write a brief explanation explaining any changes you have made. Remember you will be asked to share the definitions in the plenary.

New worlds: Annotated text

In search of the [1]true explorer

1 Emotive adjective – suggests the writer has a view about existing definitions of 'explorer'.
3 Opening paragraph – presents an outdated image of an explorer.
5 Repetition of pronoun and use of present tense – underlines writer's attitude.
7 'Indiana Jones' – reference illustrates the 'caricature'.
9 Clear statement of opinion.
11 Noun phrase refers to earlier image of explorer – 'genuinely' suggests the writer's judgement.
13 Expert opinion.
15 Rhetorical question.

[2, 3]Think of an explorer and the image that typically springs to mind depicts a man in a pith helmet [4]sweating his way through the undergrowth, a troupe of overburdened porters trailing behind him. [5]He's most likely wearing khaki, probably in the tropics and almost definitely Victorian. He's [6]certainly a man and always white.

This caricature, which is gradually evolving into someone resembling [7]Indiana Jones has been branded on our subconscious. [8]It's a powerful, defining image, but as a portrayal of someone at the forefront of discovery, [9]it is clearly incorrect.

[10]For a start, it suggests that the process of discovery peaked long ago, with Livingstone and Stanley perhaps. But the truth is, when it comes to exploration, we're still literally skimming the surface. Caver Andrew Eavis, for example, has discovered not only more physical terrain than anyone alive, but also more of what was [11]genuinely unknown than most of the [11]great trailblazers of yesteryear.

[12]And according to [13]astronaut Edwin 'Buzz' Aldrin, we still have better maps of the surface of the moon than of the sea floor. The sea is the world's largest habitat,[14] "home to the least-understood members of the web of life," says deep-sea zoologist Dr Julian Partridge.

[12]So [15]why does the outdated image of the explorer linger? [8]It's a legacy from a time when whole swathes of territory were being revealed. The Victorian explorers were the heroes of their day. Exploration was something that happened not in a laboratory but in some godforsaken wilderness.

The most famous moment in the history of exploration is not the Russian Yuri Gagarin's launch into space – the first time man had escaped the bounds of our planet – but the finding of a 'lost' explorer by Stanley: "Dr Livingstone, I presume." The two men captured our imagination by greeting each other with a civilised handshake, symbolically uniting in the heart of the Dark Continent.

I asked a [16]range of those whom we might think of as today's leading explorers how they define the word. According to Sir Ranulph Fiennes, [17]who the *Guinness Book of Records* dubbed the "greatest living explorer", an explorer is "someone who has done something that no human has done before and also done something scientifically useful".

One of the leading mountaineers of the postwar generation, Sir Chris Bonington, feels exploration is to be found in the act of physically touching the unknown. "You have to have gone somewhere new," he says.

[18]So, with the Victorian image of the heroic trailblazer reaching its use-by date, it would appear that it's time to widen the definition of an explorer. A worthy place to start is in the sciences, [19]where the bounds of knowledge are being pushed back daily. Astronomers are using ever-larger and more sensitive telescopes to examine the farthest reaches of the cosmos, in effect looking billions of years back in time. [20]Meanwhile, their colleagues are investigating the solar system, using remote-controlled probes to capture unprecedented images from the surface of Mars and beyond.

[21]It seems that exploration is all about pushing back or examining a frontier of knowledge and then imparting the new information.

2 Direct appeal to readers – introduces topic sentence.
4 Unflattering description of explorer – suggesting the porters did all the work.
6 Emphatic statement conveys key features of 'Victorian' values.
8 Impersonal 'It's' adds weight to the argument.
10 Informal linking phrase – indicates the first of several points.
12 'And'/'So' coordinating connectives link paragraphs and link argument.
14 Quotation from an expert to add weight to the argument.
16 Suggests a wide choice – underlines the earlier point about modern exploration.
17 Quotations from famous explorers widens the definition and supports the writer's own views.
18 Subordinating connective to front clause – informal/conversational – links the writer's opinion, his findings, with the forthcoming conclusion.
19 Suggestive of time and research moving on rapidly.
20 Temporal connective.
21 Passive construction to add authenticity – impersonal – wide agreement with his views adds more weight to his conclusion.

23 Underlines importance of these human qualities. Infinitive verb form 'to' underlines the key points.

[22]We are all explorers. Our desire [23]to discover and to share our new-found knowledge are part of being human and have played a vital role in our success as a species.

By Benedict Allen from *Geographical*

22 Emphatic definition – short statement for effect – supported by 'our' to include reader and all of humanity.

14 Moving about

Introduction

The three texts in this unit consider the role of transport in our society.

 Henry Ford  Driving Miss Phoebe  Transport 2000

Reading strategies

- make judgements
- establish a relationship with the writer
- empathise
- infer

Assessment focuses and framework objectives

Select the appropriate objectives for your class from the lists below, grouped by assessment focus.

Assessment focus 2 – understand, describe, select or retrieve information, events or ideas from texts and use quotation and reference to text

Year 7	Year 8	Year 9
• **R2 Extract information**	• **R2 Independent research**	• R1 Information retrieval

Assessment focus 3 – deduce, infer or interpret information, events or ideas from texts

Year 7	Year 8	Year 9
• **R8 Infer and deduce**	• R7 Implied and explicit meanings	• **W7 Layers of meaning**

Assessment focus 5 – explain and comment on the writer's use of language, including grammatical and literary features at text level

Year 7	Year 8	Year 9
• R13 Non-fiction style • R14 Language choices	• W12 Formality and word choice • R7 Implied and explicit meanings • R11 Compare treatments of same theme	• **R7 Compare texts** • **R12 Rhetorical devices**

Assessment focus 6 – identify and comment on writers' purposes and viewpoints and the overall effect of the text on the reader

Year 7	Year 8	Year 9
• R9 Distinguish writer's views	• **R5 Trace developments** • R6 Bias and objectivity • R11 Compare treatments of same theme	• R11 Author's standpoint

Moving about: Sample lesson plan

Driving Miss Phoebe

Questions 1–2: page 138 of the Pupils' Book

Assessment focus 5 – explain and comment on the writer's use of language, including grammatical and literary features at text level

Year 7	Year 8	Year 9
• R13 Non-fiction style • R14 Language choices	• W12 Formality and word choice • R7 Implied and explicit meanings • R11 Compare treatments of same theme	• **R7 Compare texts**

10 Starter

1 Explain to pupils that they will be exploring the advantages and disadvantages of using different modes of transport to travel to school: being driven in a car, using public transport or walking. Ask pupils to work in groups of three. Give each group one minute to discuss and record the advantages and disadvantages for each aspect of travel to school.

2 Ask one person from each group to act as an envoy, sharing ideas with another group. Ensure that members of each group record any new ideas they receive.

20 Introduction

1 Explain to the class that they will be reading a humorous article on the advantages and disadvantages of doing a school run.

2 Using an OHT of the section starting '*Twelve years …*' down to '*… watch ER for me*', do a shared reading with pupils. Draw out authorial voice and the types of humour used in the text. (See the annotated text on page 94). For example, in paragraph one, look at the use of exaggeration '*a billion dropped crisps*' and the use of ellipsis to build up to the punch-line. Also, the repetition of the idea of a bad smell emphasises the humorous aspect of the school run as does the use of self-deprecation '*I must be mad.*'

3 Refer to the annotated text to draw out examples of irony, self-deprecation, exaggeration and the use of rhetorical devices.

Display these terms on a flip chart as you identify them so that pupils can use them as a checklist in the development part of the lesson. Also in preparation for the development of the lesson, clarify the terms: informal, colloquialism, aside and parenthesis. Model the use of these techniques in paragraph three.

Development

1 Ask pupils to close read the rest of the text.

2 Working in pairs, ask pupils to find another example from the checklist of humorous techniques that the writer has used. They should make brief notes to indicate what the effect of the technique is on the reader.

3 Working in pairs, ask pupils to consider how the writer achieves an informal tone in the piece. They should look for examples of the following: colloquialisms, asides, parenthesis and punctuation. Again, they should make brief notes of the effect on the reader. Encourage pupils to consider how the writer uses humour to convey her feelings and attitudes and to prepare for feedback of ideas in the plenary.

5 Guided work with a group needing further support. The focus will be on the types of humour used.

Plenary

1 Ask pupils to feedback on how the writer uses humour to convey her feelings and attitudes and the techniques she uses to achieve an informal tone.

Moving about: Guided reading planner

Driving Miss Phoebe

Questions 1–2: page 138 of the Pupils' Book

Assessment focus 5 – identify and comment on the structure and organisation of texts, including grammatical and presentational features at text level

Year 7	Year 8	Year 9
• R13 Non-fiction style • R14 Language choices	• W12 Formality and word choice • R7 Implied and explicit meanings • R11 Compare treatments of same theme	• **R7 Compare texts**

Guided session

Introduction to the text	• Tell pupils that they are going to focus on the use of humour in the rest of the text. Read through the checklist of techniques with them, asking them to recall an example from the shared reading.
Strategy check	• Tell pupils that they are going to use skills of **inference**. Explain that when writers use humour, the literal meaning is often not the real meaning and that you have to read between the lines to find the meaning and look for what is being implied rather than made explicit. Say that the choice of words and how they are organised are ways writers can suggest different meanings. Give an example of how irony can operate in this way. • Explain that you will also be trying to **establish a relationship with the writer** and **hear a reading voice** and consider what this 'voice' suggests to us about the writer's thoughts and feelings.
Independent reading and related task	• Ask pupils to work in pairs and read the sections '*Who'd choose to walk?*' and '*How about a donkey?*'. Ask pupils to note any examples of humour that they can find. Remind them to refer back to the checklist of: irony, self-deprecation, exaggeration and the use of rhetorical devices. • For extra support, pick out words and phrases and ask pupils what technique they think is being used.
Return to the text: developing response	• Ask pupils to share as a group the words and phrases that they have identified and discuss the techniques that have been used. They should refer to the checklist of terms and be encouraged to give evidence and explain the effect of the technique on the reader.
Review	• Ask pupils to review the reading strategy used. Pose the question: how does the writer manage to make a serious point in a humorous way? How does the voice of the writer come through? Refer to the annotated text on page 94 to support and scaffold pupil understanding as required.

Driving Miss Phoebe

Question 2: page 138 of the Pupils' Book

Context

As a whole group we have:

- Identified techniques that writers use to convey humour, including the use of irony and exaggeration.
- Found examples of these techniques in the text.
- Commented on the effect of these techniques on the reader.

Objectives

- Explore the way that the writer uses language to convey her sense of humour.

Reading strategies

- **Infer**
  Interpret what the writer is saying. Look for what is being implied rather than being made explicit.
- **Hear a reading voice**
  How do we know the writer has a light-hearted view of the school run? Look at her choice of words and identify the humorous techniques that she uses to suggest this more light-hearted approach.

Your task

1 Work in pairs. Close read the rest of the text. Identify further examples of humorous techniques used. Use the checklist displayed on the flip chart to remind you of the techniques you should be looking for. For each example that you identify, comment on the meaning that is implied and the effect it has on the reader.

2 Still working in pairs, discuss how the writer achieves an informal tone in the article. Identify the use of:

- colloquialisms (expressions used in everyday speech)
- asides (words spoken to the reader)
- parenthesis
- punctuation.

3 Individually, reflect on the following questions:

a What impression do we get of the relationship between mother and daughter? How is this conveyed through the use of humour? Think about:

- The importance of having a sense of humour.
- How the situation described in this text might compare with the parent's own childhood.

b What impression do we get of the writer – can you hear a reading voice?

4 Be prepared to feedback your ideas in the plenary.

Driving Miss Phoebe

12 years of stale crisps, dog poo and war on the back seat ... but Jenny Eclair still loves driving her daughter.

Twelve years, two Golfs, a Daimler and a Polo, three wing mirrors, a million quaint Anglo Saxon swear words, thousands of mouldy apple cores and a [1]billion dropped crisps [2]... You can always tell which is the school-run car by its smell. [3]At times, my various cars have smelt very bad indeed – so much so that my daughter regularly used to faint on her way to nursery school.

That's when it started, when she was two and her kindergarten was at the top of a very steep hill. I could have wheeled her up in her buggy, but, [4]let's face it, I'd have had to keep sitting down for a rest and she wouldn't have got there till lunchtime. So, I drove her, and I'm still driving her.

[5]I must be mad. She's 14, she has two working legs ([6]albeit skinny ones), [7]surely she could walk? [8]Walk! She's a teenager; teenage girls can't walk. They haven't got any muscle tone – all they do is watch television. [9]They're like jellyfish with blackheads. Mine is so lazy she recently turned round and said, "Mum. I'm tired. Will you watch *ER* for me?"

1 Exaggeration adds humour.

3 Repetition of idea of bad smell builds up humour.

2 Ellipsis builds up to the punch-line.

4 Colloquial style – includes the reader.

5 Self-deprecation adds humour.

7 Use of question reinforces colloquial tone.

9 Simile to add humour.

6 Parenthesis adds humorous aside.

8 Single word sentence for effect implies strength of feeling.

Who'd choose to walk?

[10]To be honest, [11]I don't blame her for not wanting to walk. I hate walking, all that putting one leg in front of another, over and over again. So tedious. [12]Anyway, it's not as if her secondary school is a nice walk away, over babbling brooks and meadows. [13]It's an urban trek, not only up a very steep hill, but down the hill and round the corner. She'd never make it. I'd put more money on a salmon.

When I was her age, I rode a bike to school. Every limb would have to have fallen off – and believe me, I tried – before my mother would have dreamt of backing her orange Mini out of the garage. Come hailstorms or blizzards, in a flapping gabardine mac, [14]my fat little knees would pump furiously a mile there and a mile back, a pocketful of sherbet lemons keeping me going.

11 Empathetic response.

13 Exaggeration for humorous effect.

10 Familiar tone.

12 Chatty style.

14 Self-deprecating humour builds amusing image of the mother.

How about a donkey?

Phoebe doesn't ride a bike; she'd have to wear a helmet, because we live in London, and that would ruin her hair! She could get a bus, if they went in vaguely the right direction – but they don't. In fact, considering the amount of [15]clobber she has to carry the only solution (apart from me giving her a lift, of course) [16]would be a donkey.

OK, I'm making excuses; we live in a rough area, she can't run very fast ...

[17]The fact is, I like taking her. The school run delivers 15 precious minutes of 'us' time, to gossip, bitch and natter. No-one else can make me laugh as much as she can before nine o'clock in the morning. And the fact that I've got a coat on over my pyjamas is irrelevant.

Actually, this current school run is a breeze – now that she is no longer three, I don't have to carry her screaming into the car (unless she's got double Physics, of course). Neither do I have to drive very far: Camberwell to Dulwich – barely gets me out of second gear ([18]yes, I'm one of 'those' drivers).

15 Informal language.

17 Honest acknowledgement of her part in this.

16 Ridiculous suggestions for humorous effect.

18 Colloquial aside makes fun of herself.

19 Exaggeration for humorous effect.

[19]Armageddon on the back seat

The worse school run was the primary school leg where, every term day for seven years, we made the seven-mile round trip from the bowels of South London over the river to [20]Chelsea! Why? Because the local schools were full of people biting each other and screaming [21](and that was the teachers).

20 Exclamation. Contrasts 'bowels of London' with upmarket Chelsea.

21 Parenthesis gives a witty aside.

It wasn't just us, either, the Chelsea run involved three other local kids, so at least the burden was shared among the parents. Ha! My partner was the only dad who ever braved it. And that's not surprising, really; we did have some nutters on board.

[22]Most days, Armageddon would break out on the back seat: "He pinched me!" "She kicked me!" In the end I discovered that I could drown them out with old punk tapes. Seven-year-olds really like John Cooper Clarke and The Clash. I'd regularly deposit them outside school chanting *London's Burning* – and it wasn't the nursery rhyme version.

22 Dialogue conveys negative aspects of school run in humorous way.

No school run is drama-free. There's always one child who climbs into the car with a heavily dog-poo-encrusted shoe; there's never anywhere to park; other mothers are bitches from hell; and I once drove over a lollipop man's foot. But at least it's all accomplished before the sun's over the yardarm.

23 Parental perspective.

The [23]dreaded disco run

Much more inconvenient is when the school run morphs into the disco run. Last month, my daughter and her cronies went to a [24]massive teenage thrash in Hammersmith: pick-up time 1.30am! Sober and exhausted, her father and I waited outside on the pavement with all the other wheyfaced parents (Sir Bob Geldof included). And all of a sudden, I regressed. I felt exactly like I had on that first day I'd picked her up from nursery: "[25]Has she had a good time? What if she comes out crying? What if a nasty boy's been mean to her?" Oh God, when does it end? I suppose when they're old enough to drive themselves.

24 Contrast teenage and adult perspectives.

25 Implies close relationship with her daughter.

The other day I remarked that, by the time she's 17, my Golf will be very clapped-out indeed and, depending on GCSE results and as long as she hasn't made me a grandmother, she just might inherit it. You should have seen her face: "Actually, Mum. I was thinking more along the lines of one of those new Minis!" "Get out," I said.

[26]Yes, the school run can indeed be a nightmare, but I will miss it.

26 Sums up the main point of the article.

From AA magazine

15 Heroes

Introduction

The texts in this unit examine the nature of heroism and its depiction in both fiction and non-fiction texts.

The coming of King Arthur

Sir Thomas More

Ellen MacArthur

Reading strategies

- see images
- infer
- deduce
- ask questions
- make judgements
- interpret patterns
- relate to previous reading experience

Assessment focuses and framework objectives

Select the appropriate objectives for your class from the lists below, grouped by assessment focus. Consider not just their year group but also their starting point for this aspect of reading and the desired focus for the teaching.

Assessment focus 3 – deduce, infer or interpret information, events or ideas from texts

Year 7	Year 8	Year 9
• R6 Active reading • **R8 Infer and deduce**	• R4 Versatile reading • R7 Implied and explicit meanings • R11 Compare treatments of same theme	• **W7 Layers of meaning** • **R7 Compare texts**

Assessment focus 4 – identify and comment on the structure and organisation of texts, including grammatical and presentational features at text level

Year 7	Year 8	Year 9
• R7 Identify main ideas	• **R10 Development of key ideas** • Sn7 Cohesion and coherence	• **R7 Compare texts** • **Sn6 Paragraph organisation**

Assessment focus 5 – explain and comment on writers' uses of language, including grammatical and literary features at word and sentence level

Year 7	Year 8	Year 9
• R13 Non-fiction style • R14 Language choices	• R7 Implied and explicit meanings	• **R7 Compare texts**

Heroes: Sample lesson plan

Compare task: page 150 of the Pupils' Book

Assessment focus 3 – deduce, infer or interpret information, events or ideas from texts

Year 7	Year 8	Year 9
• R6 Active reading • **R8 Infer and deduce**	• R4 Versatile reading • R7 Implied and explicit meanings • R11 Compare treatments of same theme	• **R7 Compare texts**

10 Starter

1 Using individual whiteboards, ask pupils, in pairs, to list the characteristics which they think are typically heroic.

2 Prioritise these in the feedback session. Try to define the nature of heroism. Ask pupils whether there is such a thing as a 'typical' hero.

15 Introduction

1 Explain that the lesson is focusing on the nature of heroism. They will be comparing the three texts they have read in order to explore whether King Arthur, Sir Thomas More or Ellen MacArthur are typical heroes.

2 Using the Ellen MacArthur text, model how to 'read between the lines' to **deduce** and **infer** the nature of Ellen MacArthur's heroic qualities from the first two paragraphs. (See annotated text on page 105.) Draw out the hints that she is remarkable for becoming 'Yachtsman of the Year' when she was brought up in Derbyshire, a 'landlocked county', etc.

20 Development

1 Put pupils in groups of four and give each group one of the three texts as their main focus. They can then select one other text to work on and will be expected to work on these two texts in detail, although they will also be expected to comment on all three. Ask each group to scan the texts in the same way as in the introduction for evidence of the heroic qualities of the characters – King Arthur, Sir Thomas More or Ellen MacArthur. Explain that they will be presenting their findings in an extended plenary to assess how and why the three characters could be considered a typical hero.

2 Explain that some of them might find it helpful to record their notes in a simple point–evidence–explanation table once their annotations have been completed. Invite pupils to work on all three texts in this way, even though they will only be expected to report back on two texts.

3 Guided group: work with a group of pupils who find the strategies **infer** and **deduce** quite challenging. This group will continue working on the Ellen MacArthur text and compare Ellen MacArthur's heroic qualities with those revealed in Sir Thomas More's letter.

15 Plenary

1 Each group contributes to a summary of the nature of the heroism shown by the three figures. Ask pupils to explain how typical these characters are as heroes.

2 As a final activity, move the discussion on to what these heroes tell us about the society in which they live or lived.

Heroes: Guided reading planner

Compare task: page 150 of the Pupils' Book

Assessment focus 3 – deduce, infer or interpret information, events or ideas from texts

Year 7	Year 8	Year 9
• R6 Active reading • **R8 Infer and deduce**	• R4 Versatile reading • R7 Implied and explicit meanings • R11 Compare treatments of same theme	• **R7 Compare texts**

Guided session

Introduction to the text	• Explain that the focus for the group will be the heroic qualities shown in both the Ellen MacArthur text and the Thomas More letter.
Strategy check	• **Deduce** and **infer** – ask pupils to explain their understanding of these strategies and how they can do this when they read: eg keep their task in mind as they find relevant information, ask questions, think about what has been included and the writer's attitude towards it, think of what might be the readers' views in the same circumstances, search for 'hidden meanings', make judgements. Draw their attention to examples from earlier in the lesson.
Independent reading and related task	• Divide the group into two: each group to focus on one of the two texts. Support those working on the Thomas More letter by working through the first few lines (see annotated text on page 103 for details). Draw out how you are 'reading between the lines' to discover the heroic qualities of Sir Thomas More just as you did with the Ellen MacArthur text. Pupils then annotate a copy of the text individually, using the grid from the lesson plan to help with their recording of information. Support pupils where necessary by highlighting significant phrases which they could focus on.
Return to the text: developing response	• Ask pupils to compare and share notes with each group reporting back on their findings. Allow pupils time to scan the texts for the relevant references which support points made about heroic qualities. Give time to record information on the table • Try to develop responses by helping pupils to articulate and expand on their ideas on the heroic qualities shown by both Ellen MacArthur and Sir Thomas More.
Review	• Review the reading strategy used and set a personal target.

Heroes: Group worksheet

Compare task: page 150 of the Pupils' Book

Context

As a whole group we have:

- Explored the qualities that a hero might have.
- Read the beginning of Text 3 about the sailor, Ellen MacArthur, searching for information which tells us about her heroic qualities.

Objectives

- Deduce the nature of each character's heroism.
- Explore the theme of heroism in contrasting texts.

Reading strategies

- **Infer**
  Look behind what the writer is saying and work out what is implied about the character as a hero.
- **Deduce**
  Here is your chance to be a 'detective' and use evidence in the text to work out hidden meanings. Look at the things the author chooses to write about. Try to work out what it says about the nature of heroism.

Your task

1 Spend six minutes working individually on the first text you have been given and six minutes on the text of your choice, searching for clues about the heroic qualities of the central character. Think back to the list of heroic qualities you came up with at the start of the unit. Do the characters in the text you are studying show any of these qualities?
Hint: Pick out relevant quotations as you read through each text. You could record these on a spider diagram, grouping the quotations by the different heroic qualities they show.

2 Now working in a group of four, compare and develop your notes. Remember you will have to report back to the whole class, so you will need to have your notes organised to include:

- the heroic qualities shown
- the quotation or reference to the text which suggests this
- your comments on the significance of this point.

You might want to make a 3-column list, organised under the following headings to help you do this. An example has been completed for you to follow:

Heroic qualities shown
Took on an exceptional challenge

A quotation which suggests this
'Will spend 100 days alone at sea'

A comment on the nature of this heroism
First female yachtsman to do this.

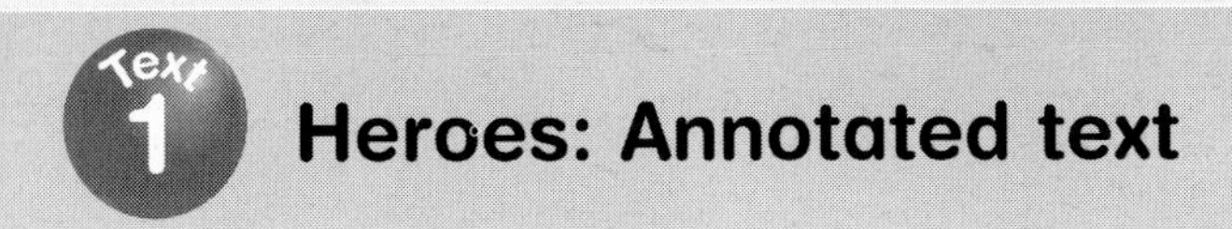

The coming of King Arthur

'O King,' she cried, 'and I will tell thee: few,
Few, but all brave, all of one mind with him;
For I was near him when the savage yells
Of Uther's peerage died, [1]and Arthur sat
Crown'd on the daïs, and his warriors cried,
"[2]Be thou the king, and we will work thy will
Who love thee." Then the King [3]in low deep tones
And simple words of great authority,
[4]Bound them by so strait vows to his own self,
That when they rose, knighted from kneeling, some
Were pale as at the passing of a ghost,
Some flush'd, and others dazed, as one who wakes
Half-blinded at the coming of a light.

'But when he spake and [5]cheer'd his Table Round
With large, divine, and comfortable words,
Beyond my tongue to tell thee – I beheld
From eye to eye thro' all their Order flash
[6]A momentary likeness of the King:
And ere it left their faces, thro' the cross
And those around it and the Crucified,
Down from the casement over Arthur, smote
Flame-colour, vert and azure, in three rays,[7]
One falling upon each of three fair queens,
Who stood in silence near his throne, the [8]friends
Of Arthur, gazing on him, tall, with bright
Sweet faces, who will help him at his need.

[9]'And there I saw mage Merlin, whose vast wit
And hundred winters are but as the hands
Of loyal vassals toiling for their liege.

'And near him stood the [10]Lady of the Lake,
Who knows a subtler magic than his own –
[11]Clothed in white samite, mystic, wonderful.
She gave the King his huge cross-hilted sword,
Whereby to drive the heathen out: [12]a mist
Of incense curl'd about her, and her face
Wellnigh was hidden in the minster gloom;
[13]But there was heard among the holy hymns
A voice as of the waters, for she dwells
Down in a deep; calm, whatsoever storms
May shake the world, and when the surface rolls,
Hath power to walk the waters like our Lord.

'There likewise I beheld Excalibur
Before him at his crowning borne, the sword
That rose from out the bosom of the lake,
And [14]Arthur row'd across and took it – rich
With jewels, elfin Urim, on the hilt,

1 Arthur has just been crowned.

2 Words of love, respect and duty from Arthur's 'warriors'.

3 Arthur speaks with dignity and in a measured manner: simply and with authority.

4 His words have various effects but all knights appear stunned and transformed.

5 Arthur takes control by reassuring and praising his knights magnanimously.

6 The knights all have the same look as their king.

7 A divine light illuminates the scene with the crucifixion at its apex, symbolising their goodness and God's approval.

8 Confirmation that he is surrounded by like-minded followers.

9 The presence of the magician Merlin confirms his approval.

10 The ceremony is also attended by the Lady of the Lake.

11 Her appearance is magnificent but delicate, almost gossamer. She gives Arthur Excalibur.

12 She is not earthly: her voice is calm and deep, she has divine qualities.

13 Her presence at the coronation signifies the importance of Arthur as King.

14 Arthur claims Excalibur as it rises from the lake.

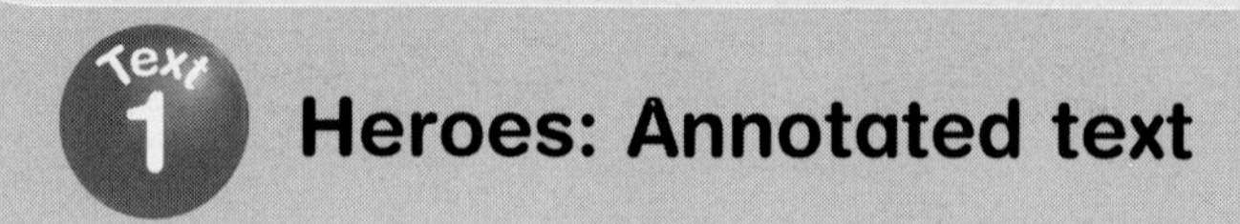

Heroes: Annotated text

Bewildering heart and eye – the blade so bright
That men are blinded by it – on one side,
Graven in the oldest tongue of all this world,
[15]"Take me," but turn the blade and ye shall see,
And written in the speech ye speak yourself,
[15]"Cast me away!" And sad was Arthur's face
Taking it, but old Merlin counsell'd him,
"[16]Take thou and strike! the time to cast away
Is yet far-off." [17]So this great brand the king
Took, and by this will beat his foemen down.'

From *Idylls of the King* by Alfred Lord Tennyson

15 Excalibur appears to have conflicting advice engraved upon it.

16 Merlin explains. Throughout his reign Arthur will be guided and counselled by Merlin's wise words.

17 Armed with Excalibur Arthur is in a position of considerable power.

Sir Thomas More

1477–1535[1]

1 A secondary historical source.

[2]Thomas More – lawyer, prolific writer, MP and statesman – was Chancellor of England between 1529 and 1532. He rose to prominence early in the 16th century as one of Henry VIII's most [3]effective and trusted civil servants, acting as the King's secretary, interpreter, speech-writer, chief diplomat, advisor and confidant.

2 The tone is factual and detached. Written in complex and compound sentences to include detail.

3 The facts included list his achievements.

At the same time More was building up a reputation as one of Europe's leading scholars. Around 1515 he wrote the *History of Richard III* which has been described as the first masterpiece of English historiography; and in 1516 published his most important work *Utopia* – a description of an imaginary communist republic ruled by reason and intended to contrast sharply with the strife-ridden reality of contemporary Europe politics.

Despite his own free-thinking, [4]More was a passionate defender of Catholic orthodoxy – writing pamphlet after pamphlet against heresy, banning and confiscating unorthodox books, and even taking personal responsibility when Chancellor for the interrogation of English heretics.

4 A highly complex sentence starting with a connective. The main clause is underlined but it is surrounded by subordinate clauses.

More took on the post of Lord Chancellor just when King Henry had become determined to obtain a divorce from Catherine of Aragon, something forbidden by church law. The previous Chancellor, Lord Wolsey, had failed to achieve this objective.

When Henry declared himself 'Supreme Head of the Church in England' – thus establishing the Anglican Church and allowing him to set aside his marriage – [5]More resigned the Chancellorship to be replaced as the King's main advisor by Thomas Cromwell. He continued to argue against the King's divorce and the split with Rome, and in 1534 was arrested after refusing to swear an Oath of Succession repudiating the Pope and accepting the annulment of the marriage to Catherine. Fifteen months later More was tried for treason at Westminster, and [6]on July 6th 1535 he was executed by beheading on Tower Hill.

5 Shows More to be a man of principle.

6 Prepared to die for his beliefs.

[7]*1535 – [8]the last letter of Thomas More*

[9, 10]Our Lord bless you, [11]good daughter, and your good husband, and your little boy, and all yours, and all my children, and [12]all my god-children and all our friends. Recommend me when ye may to my good daughter Cecily, whom I beseech Our Lord to comfort; and I send her my blessing and to all her children, and [13]pray her to pray for me. [14]I send her a handkercher, and God comfort my good son, her husband. My good daughter Daunce hath the picture in parchment that you delivered me from my Lady Coniers, her name on the back. Show her that [15]I heartily pray her that you may send it in my name to her again, for a token from me to pray for me.

I cumber you, good Margaret much, [16]but I would be sorry if it should be any longer than to-morrow, for it is St Thomas's even, and the utas of St Peter; and therefore, to-morrow long I to go to God. It were a day very meet and convenient for me.

[17]I never liked your manner towards me better than when you kissed me last; for I love when daughterly love and dear charity hath no leisure

7 A primary historical source.

8 Information that presents a moving context.

9 The tone is kind and affectionate.

10 Sets the religious context.

11 He chooses to praise them for their goodness, despite his predicament.

12 The general introduction includes all his loved ones then moves on to special members of the family.

13 Again reinforces their Christian faith.

14 A touching little gift.

15 Another gift of a picture.

16 He is prepared for his death. His faith in God gives him strength.

17 Sincere expression of affection towards his daughter.

to look to worldly courtesy. [18]Farewell, my dear child, and pray for me, and I shall for you and all your friends, [19]that we may merrily meet in heaven. I thank you for your great cost. I pray you at time convenient recommend me to my good son John More. Our Lord bless him and his good wife, my loving daughter, to whom I pray him to be good, as he hath great cause; and that, [20]if the land of mine come to his hands, he break not my will concerning his sister Daunce. And the Lord bless Thomas and Austin, and all that they shall have.[21]

From BBC history website

18 This is his formal goodbye to his family and the world.

19 Absolute faith that they will all meet again 'merrily'.

20 Suggests that John might inherit More's estate but that Daunce is also a beneficiary.

21 No mention of suffering or regret.

0105

[1]Ellen MacArthur

You can make it happen

There would be nothing remarkable in Derbyshire producing a Hill Walker of the Year or even a Potholer of the Year. But for [2]this landlocked county to produce Yachtsman of the Year, and for that award to go to a [3]22-year-old slip of a girl from Whatstandwell, is nothing short of miraculous.

Ellen MacArthur does not come from any yachting club, 'Howard's Way' culture and has not risen through the ranks of the sailing elite. As she cheerfully puts it: "I'm not a cool racing person with the right designer gear." [4]For Cowes and Hamble, substitute Flash Dam and Ogston Reservoir. Her great-grandparents came from Skye and were boating people and a great-uncle ran away to sea when young, [5]but any real connection with the sea is tenuous. When Ellen was eight, an aunt took her sailing on the east coast, after which [6]she was hooked.

At school, [6]she saved up all her dinner money for three years to buy her first boat, an eight-foot dinghy. [6]She was a "geek", she says candidly, [6]spending all her spare time reading sailing books in the library and soaking up information like a sponge. She was going to be a vet but a bout of glandular fever while she was in the Sixth Form set her back. Instead, she resolved to become a professional sailor.

[7]So at 18, she sailed single-handed round Britain and won the Young Sailor of the Year award for being the youngest person to pass the Yachtmaster Offshore Qualification, with the highest possible marks. The nautical establishment looked on benignly at [8]"Little Ellen" from Derbyshire, just 5' 2" tall, and metaphorically patted her on the head. She wrote 2,500 letters to potential sponsors – and [9]received just two replies.

They stopped patting her on the head and looked at her in a new light when she undertook the Mini-Transat solo race from Brest in France to Martinique in the French Caribbean in 1997. [10]With little money, no major sponsorship and not even a return ticket, she took the ferry to France, bought Le Poisson, a 21ft yacht, and refitted it on site. [10]She learned French in order to deal with French shipwrights and camped next to Le Poisson while she worked on the mast and hull.

[11]Then she sailed 2,700 miles across the Atlantic, a race which she completed in 33 days. This achievement brought her first major sponsorship from Kingfisher, [11]who believe in backing young people with an ambition to succeed. In a new boat, the 50 ft Kingfisher, she undertook the Route du Rhum transatlantic race in November of last year, winning her class and finishing fifth overall.

[12]She is a heroine in France, where she has been named 'La Jeune Espoire de la Voile' (Sailing's Young Hope). [12]More people flock down to the quayside to see her off on a race than fill Wembley Stadium for a Cup Final. They shout her favourite phrase, "Ellen à donf" which means "Full on! Go for it". Sailing in France is what the marine industry hopes will arrive in Britain, where water sports appeal to a wider audience, especially young people.

1 The challenge is directed at the reader. It instantly involves us, suggesting we can be like her.

2 This makes her extraordinary.

3 Suggests frailty: a mere girl.

4 She gained her experience on a reservoir near her home.

5 This phrase encapsulates the whole paragraph, suggesting she must have extraordinary qualities to have succeeded as a yachtswoman.

6 All suggest her enthusiasm, determination and ambition.

7 Early success showed her potential as a sailor.

8 She was patronised by the nautical establishment.

9 No early support or encouragement.

10 She was prepared to overcome all obstacles.

11 This success brought sponsorship as her 'ambition to succeed' was recognised.

12 International appeal. Her reputation has spread. She is a big sporting celebrity in France.

Heroes: Annotated text

13 Electronic communication means that the world can follow her progress and she can keep in touch.

[13]Thousands follow Ellen's race progress on the Internet. Messages and digital pictures from a boat in the middle of the Atlantic can be instantly relayed around the world from the onboard computer and updated every hour. Satellite phones mean contact on shore for weather routing and emergencies. Ellen's uncle, Dr Glyn MacArthur, a GP in Crich, was woken during one night to hear Ellen's voice asking his advice on a head injury she'd sustained during a severe gale on the Route du Rhum.

Exhausting racing conditions mean [14]sleeping in ten-minute snatches, a survival suit that doesn't come off for a week at a time and hands and wrists covered in salt sores and cuts. Dehydrated food comes in packets: if they get wet, the labels peel off and she doesn't know if she'll be eating curry or pudding until she opens one. [14]Sails, weighing twice as much as she does, may need changing a dozen times a day.

14 Several examples of the hardships she has to endure. This suggests she is tough and resourceful.

15 The good times.

There are moments of pure elation – [15]sunrises and seascapes that take the breath away. But there are nightmare times when lone sailors must become engineers.

[16]She describes a night and day that ran together, when 15 litres of fluid (resembling cooking oil) burst from the rams controlling the keel, the big steel fin that goes down through the boat. In heavy seas, slipping and sliding round the deck and with the keel unstabilised, she had to drip feed oil back in to the reservoir through a tiny funnel. Before she'd fixed the keel, a piece on one of the sails ripped, which meant taking down the sail and sewing for five hours through the night. Water came through the hatch and was swilling round the boat. And then later, when she'd dried all the compartments, a mighty bang threw the boat on to its side and all the electricity that powered the satcom communication system went off.

16 a detailed anecdote of one nightmare scenario.

17 Ellen's own testimony personalises this whole text. We are permitted to hear her thoughts and feelings.

[17]What keeps her going is sheer determination not to be beaten: "When it's a race, you just can't stop. Five times a day, you get the position of all the other boats in the race and work out whether you've gained or lost time," she says. "It would be easy to say, 'chill out', when you're tired but you never have to lose the goal of the finish line. [18]That's what you set out to do and that's what you stick to."

18 A strong competitive instinct and absolute determination drive her onwards in a race.

From www.ellenmacarthur.com

16 Places worth saving

Introduction

The three texts in this unit deal with the subject of conservation.

 Ancient coral reefs under attack

 The Galapagos

 Going, Going

Reading strategies

- establish a relationship with the author
- make judgements
- reinterpret
- see images
- deduce
- predict what will happen
- relate to previous reading experience
- establish a relationship with the writer
- empathise

Assessment focuses and framework objectives

Select the appropriate objectives for your class from the lists below, grouped by assessment focus.

Assessment focus 3 – deduce, infer or interpret information, events or ideas from texts

Year 7	Year 8	Year 9
• R6 Active reading • **R8 Infer and deduce**	• R4 Versatile reading • R6 Bias and objectivity • R7 Implied and explicit meanings	• W7 Layers of meaning • R4 Evaluate information

Assessment focus 5 – explain and comment on writers' uses of language, including grammatical and literary features at word and sentence level

Year 7	Year 8	Year 9
• **R12 Character, setting and mood** • R14 Language choices	• W11 Figurative vocabulary • R14 Literary conventions	• **R12 Rhetorical devices**

Assessment focus 6 – identify and comment on writers' purposes and viewpoints and the overall effect of the text on the reader

Year 7	Year 8	Year 9
• R16 Author attitudes	• R11 Compare treatments of the same theme	• R6 Authorial perspective • R10 Interpretations of text • R11 Author's standpoint

Assessment focus 7 – relate texts to their social, cultural and historical contexts and literary traditions

Year 7	Year 8	Year 9
• R19 Poetic form	• R16 Cultural context	• **R16 Different cultural contexts**

Places worth saving: Sample lesson plan

Going, Going

Question 1–3: page 159 of the Pupils' Book

Assessment focus 5 – explain and comment on writers' uses of language, including grammatical and literary features at word and sentence level

Year 7	Year 8	Year 9
• **R12 Character, setting and mood** • R14 Language choices	• W11 Figurative vocabulary • R14 Literary conventions	• **R12 Rhetorical devices**

Assessment focus 7 – relate texts to their social, cultural and historical contexts and literary traditions

Year 7	Year 8	Year 9
• R19 Poetic form	• R16 Cultural context	• **R16 Different cultural contexts**

Starter

1. Present the poem and introduce the idea of texts being a product of their time and place.
2. Provide some details of Larkin's life. (Lived 1922–1985, a university librarian in Hull, poetry, often about urban deprivation.) Then present the following quotation: **'(Larkin) ...addressed everyday British life in plain, straightforward language...his language was plain, his approach cool...'**

   Explain that this is a critic writing about Larkin. Ask pupils to scan the poem to find 'plain straightforward language.' Ask pupils to substitute alternatives for these examples, such as *'before I snuff it'*. Explain that the technique of trying out alternatives can often help to develop understanding of the poem's meaning.

Introduction

1. Ask pupils to read the poem through once quickly, then a second time more slowly, writing down their first reactions. For pupils not used to this technique, present these prompts as guidance:
   - What I think the poem might be about
   - What I can't understand
   - Words or phrases that interest me
   - Sum up what the poet is trying to say
   - Whether or not I like what I'm reading.

Development

1. Compare reading a poem with looking at a picture: at first you see the whole picture; gradually you start to see the details. Explain that test questions are often either 'wide-angled' questions looking at the poem as a whole or more 'closely-focused' questions examining specific details.
2. Ask pupils to work through the activities on page 159 of the Pupils' Book. Work with higher-attaining pupils in the guided group and ask the remainder of the class to work in pairs.

Plenary

1. Recap differences between wide-angle and closely-focused questions. Return to the earlier 'reaction papers' and ask pupils to consider how their reactions to the poem have changed. Explain that this **re-interpretation** of the text is a key strategy for understanding it.

Places worth saving: Guided reading planner

Going, Going

Questions 1–3: page 159 of the Pupils' Book

Assessment focus 5 – explain and comment on writers' uses of language, including grammatical and literary features at word and sentence level

Year 7	Year 8	Year 9
• **R12 Character, setting and mood** • R14 Language choices	• W11 Figurative vocabulary • R14 Literary conventions	• **R12 Rhetorical devices**

Assessment focus 7 – relate texts to their social, cultural and historical contexts and literary traditions

Year 7	Year 8	Year 9
• R19 Poetic form	• R16 Cultural context	• **R16 Different cultural contexts**

Guided session

Introduction to the text	• Talk pupils briefly through the answers to questions 1a, 2a and 3a in the Pupils' Book. Remind pupils that these are wide-angled questions, designed to give them an overview of the poem.
Strategy check	• Remind pupils of the idea of a developing response – ask pupils to think of a digital camera picture when you press 'zoom'; gradually the selected details of the picture become much clearer and you begin to see the whole rather differently. Link this to the reading strategy **Reinterpret** and check pupil understanding of how and when to use this strategy.
Independent reading and related task	• Now model the answer to question 1b, drawing attention to the need for close reference to the text supported by accurate and brief quotations. • Ask pupils to tackle question 2b orally and to present their answers to the group. Question 3b should then be answered briefly in writing. • Now look at question 1c and ask pupils to consider in what ways it is different from 1a and 1b. Explain to pupils how question 1 starts looking at three verses of the poem, then focuses on a specific line, before looking in detail at word level. Ask the group to work in pairs to formulate a response to the question.
Return to the text: developing response	• Still working in pairs, ask pupils to write a 'wide-angled' question about the poem focusing on the theme of the poem and a closely-focused question looking at a specific detail from the poem. For homework, ask pupils to answer someone else's question and to evaluate how useful they thought the question was in helping them to understand the poem better.
Review	• Recap the strategy pupils have used and the question types they have encountered.

Places worth saving: Group worksheet

Going, Going

Questions 1–3: page 159 of the Pupils' Book

Context

As a whole group we have:

- Looked at how to read a poem quickly to get the sense of what it is about and why it is written in the way that it is and to **re-read** in more detail, developing new interpretations.
- Explored the difference between wide-angled and closely-focused examination questions.

Objectives

- Build up understanding of the themes of the poem and the poet's point of view.
- Identify different types of questions ('wide-angled' and 'closely-focused') and be able to answer these appropriately.

Reading strategy

- **Reinterpret**
  Think about how your ideas about the themes of the poem are changing. Do you feel and think the same as you did initially as you work through the questions?

Your task

1. Begin by reading and answering questions 1a, 2a and 3a (page 160 of the Pupils' Book). These questions each focus on three stanzas from the poem and are wide-angle questions. This means the questions ask you to give a response based on your reading of the whole poem – drawing on your knowledge and ideas of the themes of the poem. Discuss your answers to questions 1a, 2a and 3a with your partner before writing them down.
2. Move on to questions 1b, 2b, 3b. These are more closely focused questions. To answer them you need to **re-read** sections of the poem very closely, focusing on details of the poet's choice of language. Work with your partner to write your answers.
3. Now work on your own to answer questions 1c, 2c and 3c.
4. Work with your partner again to answer the following question: what do questions 1c, 2c and 3c have in common, and how are these questions different from the earlier ones?

Places worth saving: Annotated text

1 Title suggests an auction sale in which the past is being sold off.
3 Poem about the narrator's personal experience.
5 Colloquialism.

[1]Going, Going

[2]I thought it would last [3]my time –
The sense that, beyond the town,
There [4]would always be fields and farms,
Where the village [5]louts could climb
Such trees as were not cut down;
I knew [6]there'd be false alarms

In the papers about old streets
And split-level shopping, but some
Have always been left so far;
And when the old part retreats
As the [7]bleak high-risers come
[8]We can always escape in the car.
Things are tougher than we are, just

As earth will always respond
However we [9]mess it about;
Chuck filth in the sea, if you must:
The tides will be clean beyond.
– [10]But what do I feel now? Doubt?
Or age, simply? The crowd
Is young in the M1 café;
Their [11]kids are screaming for [12]more –
More houses, more parking allowed,
More caravan sites, more pay.[13]
On the Business Page, a score

[14]Of spectacled grins approve
Some takeover bid that entails
Five per cent profit (and ten
Per cent more in the estuaries): move
Your works to the unspoilt dales
([15]Grey area grants)! And when

You try to get near the sea
In summer ...[16]
It seems, just now,
To be happening so very fast;
Despite all the land left free
[17]For the first time I feel somehow
That it isn't going to last,

That before I [18]snuff it, the whole
[19]Boiling will be bricked in
Except for the tourist parts –
First slum of Europe: a role
It won't be so hard to win,
With a cast of [20]crooks and tarts.

2 Poem is punctuated by the poet's reflections on the situation he is describing.
4 Conditional tense – the future that might happen.
6 Contraction is informal, the writer talking directly to the reader, informally.
7 Evocative description – personifying the blocks of flats.
8 'I' has changed to 'we', not just the poet that is being affected.
9 Informal language.
10 Three questions in succession – poet is trying to explain precisely what he is feeling.
11 Very disparaging of other people, unsympathetic to their lives.
12 Repetition of 'more'.
13 Poet does not accept their right to want these things.
14 Describing people as if they were objects, dehumanised.
15 Making a joke – not 'green field' sites.
16 Left unfinished, the reader left to speculate.
17 Very tentative 'somehow' reflects a growing doubt.
18 Informal language.
19 1950s slang.
20 Very disparaging of other people.

Places worth saving: Annotated text

And that will be England gone,
The [21]shadows, the meadows, the lanes,
The guildhalls, the carved choirs.
There'll be books; it will linger on
In galleries; but all that remains
For us will be concrete and tyres.

Most things are never meant.
[22]This won't be, most likely: but [23]greeds
And garbage are too thick-strewn
To be swept up now, or invent
[24]Excuses that make them all needs.
I [25]just think it will happen, soon.

By Philip Larkin

21 'S' sounds at the ends of the words soften the romantic picture of a rural England.

22 Informal, almost chatty style.

23 Alliteration used for emphasis.

24 We turn our desires into needs, believing we have to have these things.

25 Use of 'just' suggests poet knows his role is not likely to be seen as important.

The natural world

Reading Booklet

The natural world

Contents

The natural world is filled with many incredible sights and wonders. From encounters with bats and snakes to the exploits of intelligent birds, nature is able to fascinate and frighten us – sometimes at the same time!

The natural world

This is an extract from a wildlife magazine. The text explores the ways in which animals such as birds can solve very complicated problems.

Clever, or what?

The BBC Natural History Unit asked you to nominate your local stars for the award of Britain's cleverest performing wild animal. The results revealed that even our most familiar animals may have a hidden flair for problem solving. Mike Beynon introduces the stars.

Driving down the M4 in heavy traffic on a hot day is not a pleasant experience. And taking a break at Membury Services is never going to be one of the great culinary experiences of your life. But for the local residents, Membury has a lot to offer. They fly around the carpark, watching fractious children and fraught parents picnic beside their cars and then tip the scraps into one of the many wastebins. This information is observed, noted and filed away for future reference.

Rooks may not be one of Britain's most charismatic birds, but they are one of our cleverest. All corvids (in Britain, this includes rooks, crows, jackdaws, ravens and choughs) have large brains relative to their body size and remarkable memories, combined with an almost aggressive inquisitiveness. Their impressive capabilities are admirably demonstrated at Membury.

Located all round the carpark are wastebins, full of tempting rubbish. The trouble is, the staff at Membury are too efficient – before the bins even start to fill to a level at which the rooks

continued 

continued 

can reach the titbits, the cleaners race to empty them. As a result, the rooks can only gaze longingly at food that is just out of beak-reach.

Or they used to. The rooks have learned to perch on the rims of bins, reach in with their beaks, grab folds of the black plastic bin liners and haul them up and over the edge. This action would, in itself, be useless. Let go, and the weight of the rubbish will pull the bin liner – and the food – back down. So, to avoid this happening, the rooks have figured out that they have to stand on the fold of bin liner they've just pulled up before reaching back down to grab another beakful. Inch by inch, the rubbish rises higher. It's a slow process, requiring immense patience – a hungry rook will have to pull out up to 20 or so folds of black plastic before it can reach its prize. By this stage, it's standing on a veritable hill of scrunched-up bin liner. Distractions are all around, but the rook is dedicated to its task and finally achieves its goal – the food is within easy reach.

The bird now faces another dilemma. Does it take just one beakful of food and fly off, allowing the rest to slide back to the bottom of the bin? Surely then the effort required would outweigh the reward? Instead, the rook reaches in and tosses the scraps over its shoulder, repeating the action again and again, until a pile of food litters the pavement behind it. Now the rook can relax and gorge itself on its well-deserved prize. *If* it can get a look in – an entourage of small birds is already busy helping themselves to a free lunch, courtesy of the rook's labours.

And so to the star of the show – for me at least. Betty is a female Caledonian crow and long-time resident at Oxford University's Behavioural Ecology Research Group. She is already famous for her extraordinary capabilities, but it isn't until you see Betty in the flesh that you really get a sense of her remarkable intelligence. The inquisitiveness, the fascination with anything new, the way she cocks her head to study a novel object, the impression that she's working things out in her head before going into action. Is this insight? Whatever you call it, Betty clearly demonstrates an intellect that goes beyond simple trial and error.

Her ability to figure things out is demonstrated by the tasks she performs. Food is placed at the bottom of a tube too deep for her to reach with her beak, inside a tiny basket with a little hoop on top. Betty is given a thin wire, about 7cm long. She picks up the wire in her beak and sticks it into the tube. She can reach the food but can't raise it to the top.

Then, extraordinarily, Betty carries the wire over to the wall, pokes its end into a little hole in the plaster, then pulls upwards with her beak. In doing this, she is fashioning a primitive hook – it may be more of a shallow bend than a true hook, but it's enough. Betty flies back to the tube, inserts the wire down the shaft and through the hoop on the basket. She pulls the wire, and up comes the basket. Triumphantly, Betty pokes her beak through the hoop, drops it to the table and eats her reward.

According to experts, this feat may make Betty the first animal, other than a human, to show a clear understanding of cause and effect and fashion a tool for a specific task using novel materials not found in the wild.

The natural world

This poem by the writer Ted Hughes describes a tractor standing in a farmer's field.

Tractor

The tractor stands frozen – an agony
To think of. All night
Snow packed its open entrails. Now a head-pincering gale,
A spill of molten ice, smoking snow,
Pours into its steel.
At white heat of numbness it stands
In the aimed hosing of ground-level fieriness.

It defied flesh and won't start.
Hands are like wounds already
Inside armour gloves, and feet are unbelievable
As if the toe-nails were all just torn off.
I stare at it in hatred. Beyond it
The copse hisses – capitulates miserably
In the fleeing, failing light. Starlings,
A dirtier sleetier snow, blow smokily, unendingly, over
Towards plantations Eastward.
All the time the tractor is sinking
Through the degrees, deepening
Into its hell of ice.

The starting lever
Cracks its action, like a snapping knuckle.
The battery is alive – but like a lamb
Trying to nudge its solid-frozen mother –
While the seat claims my buttock-bones, bites
With the space-cold of earth, which it has joined
In one solid lump.

continued

continued 

I squirt commercial sure-fire
Down the black throat – it just coughs.
It ridicules me – a trap of iron stupidity
I've stepped into. I drive the battery
As if I were hammering and hammering
The frozen arrangement to pieces with a hammer
And it jabbers laughing pain-crying mockingly
Into happy fife.

And stands
Shuddering itself full of heat, seeming to enlarge slowly
Like a demon demonstrating
A more-than-usually-complete materialization –
Suddenly it jerks from its solidarity
With the concrete, and lurches towards a stanchion
Bursting with superhuman well-being and abandon
Shouting Where Where?

Worse iron is waiting. Power-lift kneels
Levers awake imprisoned deadweight,
Shackle-pins bedded in cast-iron cow-shit.
The blind and vibrating condemned obedience
Of iron to the cruelty of iron,
Wheels screeched out of their night-locks –

Fingers
Among the tormented
Tonnage and burning of iron

Eyes
Weeping in the chloroform
And the tractor, streaming with sweat
Raging and trembling and rejoicing.

By Ted Hughes

The natural world

This text is an article written by a bat expert, Adrian Hillman, who travels around the world to study bats. Here he tells of a frightening experience he had when working in a cave in Thailand.

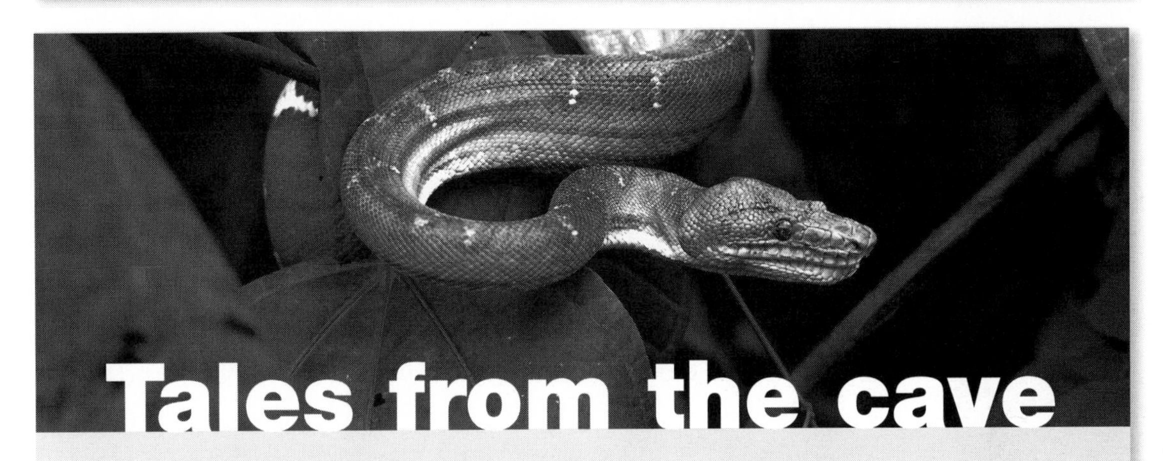

Tales from the cave

Even when I was out of sight of the cave, I sometimes knew when the bats were leaving because they took their smell out with them. All my clothes had absorbed their unique aroma, but this was a small price to pay for living next door to two and a half million bats.

Working at a bat cave 160km west of Bangkok was certainly a change from trying to persuade home-owners in England that their small pipistrelle colony wasn't really a problem. My role was to help educate both locals and tourists about the importance of protecting this immense and beneficial colony. As I used to explain, the fact that they turned insect pests into fertilizer for nothing was a service to be valued.

On this particular day I was deep inside the cave mouth, and down below me were thousands of wrinkled-lipped bats swirling around and around, as if warming up for the night's hunting. I was trying for a new angle for the video we were making and had perched myself on a relatively comfortable ledge about five metres down inside a large hole in the cave roof. Within minutes, the first few bats flew past me and out into the late afternoon sunshine, and this trickle quickly became a thick continuous column. This living river sometimes reached a rate of more than 1,000 bats a second.

As I was watching this mass exodus, something above me caught my eye. I looked up just in time to see a reticulated python wrapping itself around a bat. Intent on subduing its prey, the snake used up one too many coils and lost its grip on the rock. Python ball plus bat briefly rolled, then bounced, then rolled again before finally coming to rest several metres away from me. The snake had not let go of its meal, and the film of this python struggling to get the bat's wings down its throat is probably the highlight of the final video.

continued

continued 

Then the bats started landing on me. During the peak fly-out, the cave mouth is too narrow for them all, and many are forced to land and start crawling. I was just another obstacle in their way, and it quickly became a lot worse than I had imagined. At one point there must have been 50 bats all trying to clamber up to my head for a better take-off. In the mayhem, flying bats were also having trouble avoiding me, but I guess the collision hurt them more than they hurt me.

A quick look told me that a carpet of crawling bodies had cut off my escape route. Squashing bats underfoot did not seem appropriate for a conservationist, particularly as any slip could send me failing 10m down to the cave below, so I covered my head and sat it out, fervently wishing that all the people who had complained about their 20 pipistrelles could see me now. For the record, not a single bat got caught in my hair.

I was forced to stay there for more than half an hour before the flow lessened sufficiently to make a getaway possible. After a shower and de-lousing session, I check the video and got quite a surprise. Still hungry after the first bat, the python must have gone for a second helping and, as before, had lost its grip on the rock. The video briefly showed the snake cartwheeling down the rock face, scattering bats as it went. I'm sure it must have ended up plunging on down into the cave below, but what I found a little chilling was how close it had come to me. Indeed, it turned out that I had been less than an arm's length away from having a three-metre reticulated python land on my lap. I'll take the bats any day.

The natural world

Answer booklet

First name

____

Last name

____

Write your answers in this booklet

Questions 1–6 are about *Clever, or what*? (pages 3–4 in the Reading booklet).

1 According to paragraph 1, identify **one** skill the writer says the animals have.

- ____________________

(1 mark)

2 In paragraph 2, why does the writer include a reference to the quality of food at Membury motorway services? Identify two statements that are true and write the letter of each in the boxes below.

A	Because he thinks they should improve the quality of the food.
B	Because it is a story about eating food.
C	To contrast our dislike of the food with the feast it provides for others.
D	Because he thinks he can cook better.

The statements I think are true are: ☐ and ☐

(1 mark)

3 In paragraph 2, what is the writer describing when he says the "local residents"?

- ____________________

(1 mark)

4 From the whole text, explain one personal opinion that the writer gives. Support your answer with a quotation from the text.

Personal opinion	**Quotation**

(1 mark)

5 Explain two reasons why the writer starts with the rooks and then tells the story of Betty.

- ____________________

  ____

- ____________________

  ____

(2 marks)

6 How does writer's use of language help to engage the interest of the reader?

You should comment on:

- the humour
- the style
- the way the writer addresses the reader.
-

(5 marks)

Questions 7–11 are about *Tractor* (pages 5–6 of the Reading booklet).

7 In stanza 1, Hughes links cold and heat in his descriptions of the snow.

Complete the following table explaining the links between cold and heat and what both of these suggest about the snow.

Quotation	Explanation of the link	What it suggests about the snow
"molten ice"		
"smoking snow"		

(2 marks)

8 From stanza 2, explain one detail that tells us that the writer is affected by the cold. Support your answer with a quotation from the text.

- ____

(1 mark)

9 From stanzas 3 and 4, find two short quotations that suggest that the way the tractor responds is like a living thing.

- ____
- ____

(2 marks)

10 From stanzas 3–6, sum up the four main stages of getting the tractor ready to work. Use one phrase or sentence for each stage. The final stage (stage 5) has been done for you.

Stage 1	
Stage 2	
Stage 3	
Stage 4	
Stage 5	*The tractor "jerks" and "lurches" as it starts to move.*

(2 marks)

11 Explain how the last two lines make an effective ending to the poem. Complete the grid to show how the information at the end of the poem links or contrasts with information given earlier in the poem.

One has been completed for you.

Quotation	**Link/contrast with the rest of the poem**
Streaming with sweat	
Raging	
Trembling	
Rejoicing	*Links with the way it "jabbers ... into happy life".*

(3 marks)

Questions 12–16 are about Tales from the cave (pages 7–8 of the Reading booklet).

12 According to paragraph 1, explain how the writer knows when bats are leaving the cave.

- ______________________________

____

(1 mark)

13 Give one reason why paragraph 1 is a good opening to the text.

- ______________________________

____

____

(1 mark)

14 From paragraph 2, explain one similarity and one difference between the writer's work with bats in England and in Bangkok.

Similarity	
Difference	

(2 marks)

15 For each of the following quotations from paragraphs 3 and 5, explain why the writer's descriptions of the bats leaving the cave are appropriate.

Living river:

- ______________________________

____

Carpet of crawling bodies:

- ______________________________

____

(2 marks)

16 What does the text reveal about the writer's attitude towards bats?

You should comment on:

- his work as a conservationist
- how he reacts when he's in the cave
- how he views the incident with the snake.

(5 marks)

Assessment focuses for the questions

		AF2 Describe, select or retrieve information, events or ideas from texts and use quotation and reference to text.	AF3 Deduce, infer or interpret information, events or ideas from texts.	AF4 Identify and comment on the structure and organisation of texts, including grammatical and presentational features at text level.	AF5 Comment on writers' uses of language, including grammatical and literary features at word and sentence level.	AF6 Identify and comment on writers' purposes and viewpoints, and the effect of the text on the reader.	
Clever, or what?	1	1					
	2					1	
	3		1				
	4					1	
	5			2			
	6				5		
	Total	**1**	**1**	**2**	**5**	**2**	**11**
Tractor	7				2		
	8		1				
	9	2					
	10			2			
				3			
	Total	**2**	**1**	**5**	**2**	**0**	**10**
Tales from the cave	12	1					
	13			1			
	14		2				
	15				2		
	16					5	
	Total	**1**	**2**	**1**	**2**	**5**	**11**
	Total	**4**	**4**	**8**	**9**	**7**	**32**

Sporting life

Reading Booklet

Sporting life

Contents

Many people enjoy sport – whether it's by taking part or just watching it on the television. For some, sport is a way of keeping fit and healthy, but others find pleasure in the way activities such as cycling and running can give a sense of achievement.

Sporting life

This is an extract from a careers guide for people who are interested in jobs in the field of sport and fitness. Here the job of a sports nutritionist is explored.

What a sports nutritionist does

'Basically, I'm an educator,' explains Helga. 'I teach athletes how to improve their diets for maximum energy and peak performance. A well-balanced diet is vital to any training programme' Helga teaches courses at a university, where she also does individual nutrition counselling. And she runs her own business as a consultant.

Each athlete has specific dietary needs, depending on the sport. In rowing or wrestling, for example, an athlete's weight must be within a certain range. To meet the requirements of a particular sport, some athletes might need to gain weight, while others need to lose it. Either way, the diet must include all the vitamins and nutrients essential for good health. 'I supply accurate information and appropriate diet plans, but it's up to the athlete to follow my advice,' Helga comments.

As she counsels individual athletes about nutrition, Helga answers a lot of questions and clarifies many popular misconceptions about food. 'People fall prey to a lot of false information. For example, many athletes believe they need to take extra vitamins, but this isn't true. There are plenty of vitamins in a healthy, well-balanced diet,' Helga stresses. 'When athletes are in training, they eat larger meals, so they usually get all the vitamins their bodies need.'

Another popular misconception involves the need for protein in athletes' diets. As Helga explains, 'Surprisingly, endurance athletes such as long-distance runners need more protein, compared to weight lifters and other strength athletes.'

Helga teaches courses in fitness and nutrition. Besides regular classroom instruction, she gives talks to sports

continued 

organizations such as swimming clubs, football and basketball teams and cycling clubs. She has also appeared on television, giving tips on nutrition.

Currently Helga is writing a book for triathletes, who compete in a race that includes cycling, swimming and running. She also writes articles about health and nutrition for various publications, including a magazine for people with physical disabilities.

'I guarantee that if readers follow the suggestions in my books and combine them with proper sports training, they'll reach their best possible performance level,' smiles Helga.

Who needs protein?

Because muscle tissue is mainly protein, many people think that eating more protein will help build up muscles. Not true, says Helga. Only vigorous training develops muscles.

When weight lifters work out, they use, or 'burn' large amounts of carbohydrate for energy. Only about 1 per cent of their energy comes from protein. Very little protein is needed to build muscle.

On the other hand, endurance athletes, such as marathon runners. burn carbohydrate and fat at first. After about two hours they use up all the carbohydrate stores in their muscles. While still burning mostly fat, they start burning some protein, which will supply as much as 5 to 10 per cent of their energy.

This is why slender, long-distance runners need to eat more foods containing protein – they're replacing the protein they burned for energy.

Carbohydrate loading

When marathon runners have completed about 80 per cent of a race, they often 'hit the wall'. This total exhaustion occurs when their muscles run out of stored carbohydrate and must rely completely on fat for energy. Under these conditions, muscles can function at only 50 per cent of their peak capacity.

'Carbohydrate loading' is an eating pattern that 'tricks' muscles into storing extra carbohydrate. If runners consume large amounts of carbohydrate with little protein or fat for three days before a marathon, their muscles can store up to 50 per cent more carbohydrate then usual. They have a better chance of completing the marathon without 'hitting the wall'.

Sporting life

This text is an extract from a holiday brochure. The holidays on offer in this brochure include mountain biking breaks around the Greek islands.

Off the beaten track

Greece remains a land of great contrast and fascination, firing the imagination and always delighting the eye. Lefkas, one of the Ionian islands, is surely its best kept secret: a magnificent mountain range surrounded by the clearest blue seas.

Almost bypassed by tourism, Lefkas remains lovely, unspoilt and uncluttered, a land of hazy sunsets, warm seas and skies The diversity of styles and influences are a constant reminder of its changing past. Exploring off the beaten track villages, secluded beaches, and historic sites can still seem like a personal discovery.

The mountains are peppered with hamlets, watch towers and windmills, while the air is heady with the aromatic scent of pine and herbs. Lefkas never ceases to impress seasoned travellers and of its main coastal villages, Nidri has retained its special character and charm.

A dramatic mountain range forms the stunning backdrop to this friendly village. A myriad of trails lead inland through lush olive and citrus groves to mountain tracks and beyond. Away from tourism within minutes, the mountains offer some of the best biking imaginable, be it meandering to the next taverna or hammering for budding world-cup downhill wannabes!

Once the day's riding is over, Nidri's nightlife always offers something for everyone. This is centred around a bustling quayside of lively bars, tavernas, and even a couple of discos to entertain the most hedonistic of holidaymakers. Yet within a few minutes' walk you can easily idle away an evening by a waterside or village taverna, soaking up traditional Greek ambience and warmth.

Perfect for lazy sunworshippers, active watersports fans and scuba divers alike, Nidri offers plenty for non-cycling friends and relatives. It's also an ideal centre for island hopping and excursions.

Operating from May through to late October, Nidri is not to be missed. It offers so much more than a suntan and a quick fix of mountain biking. Its capacity for surprise year after year, as we discover exciting new tracks, together with warmth, hospitality and atmosphere, make it a mountain biking holiday to relish.

continued

continued 

Nidri: A typical week

There's so much to see from the saddle. Most rides are split to suit ability and contain enough variations to keep all standards of rider happy. Everyone meets at pre-arranged points for drinks, lunches or excursions.

MONDAY

Discover hidden Greece. A gentle leg stretch ride through shady olive groves to lunch in a sleepy hamlet. More of the same in the afternoon; the day is completed with a plunge into the deep blue waters.

TUESDAY

Bike and beach. Single tracks, dry river beds, loose and steep climbs . . . that's whetted the keenies' appetite . . . or simply cruise off-road at a sensible pace to a secluded taverna and an optional afternoon ride along a scenic coastal trail.

WEDNESDAY

Enjoy the freedom and please yourself. Discover beach windmills, ride the superb island coastal route and explore more of the 'real' Greece on Lefkas, or take the ferry to the neighbouring islands.

THURSDAY

Into the hills. Riding into the mountains – picturesque villages, historical sites and views a-plenty. Picnic lunch at a deserted monastic ruin followed by a spectacular downhill.

FRIDAY

Now for something different . . . A Caique sail to Meganissi with your bike. Explore quintessential Greek villages and deserted trails. Lunch in another unspoilt traditional taverna. Swim in crystal clear waters. Catch the boat and relax with a chilled beer on the way home.

SATURDAY

The ultimate high. Biking doesn't come better than this. The island's best trails are rolled into one awesome day you'll never forget. There's never been an opportunity to try so many bikes in their natural habitat. A real MTB treat!

Sporting life

Ian Stafford, a sports journalist, has challenged the top athletes in a variety of sports to let him compete against them. Here he is about to take part in a steeplechase in Kenya against some of the best middle-distance runners in the world.

The race of my life

We were then ordered to stand in a wide line whilst our names were introduced to the crowd. Finally, they came to me. 'And now, from London, England, please welcome Ian Stanford.'

I raised my hand and waved, feeling a little like Forrest Gump. A few weeks before this same figure had been seen kicking a football with Romario. A few days before he had been witnessed on a squash court with the greatest player in the sport's history. Now he was lining up with some of the best Kenyan athletes. People observing photographs might have come to the conclusion that my head had been superimposed on to someone else's body. But no, it was me, on every occasion. Besides, nobody else had a body like mine.

We lined up in an arched row at the start of the race. I managed to secure lane two and began to jog up and down on the spot, puffing my cheeks out and wringing my hands out and down by my side, as if they were wet. This, so I had often observed, is what athletes do moments before they run. The starter raised his gun and we all crouched low, with our arms raised upwards as if they created a tactical advantage.

BANG. I started quicker than I intended, carried along by the rush of Kenyan feet around me. For 100 metres I stayed with the pack, but I knew I would have to slow down if I stood any chance of completing the race.

We ran around a complete circuit before the first barrier came upon us. By now I had already dropped back to a more comfortable pace and I found myself lagging some 20 metres behind. If the crowd were expecting something special from this top European athlete, they soon realised this would not be the day.

Their next surprise of the day occurred seconds later. I ran towards the first barrier with intent, before producing a rugby-style side-step which sent me around and past the barrier. A large gasp was audible, followed by laughter.

I reproduced this action at the second barrier. This time another section of the crowd had a closer view of this strange *mzungu's* tactics. They had never seen a 3,000 metres steeplechase final before where one of the athletes was deliberately omitting to jump the barriers.

The water jump was always going to provide the major point of interest. The crowd was particularly deep at this barrier, in the hope that a few splash landings would be on show. I had inspected the water jump with great

continued

continued 

suspicion before the race. The dirty brown water looked deep and uninviting, and I was sure there were creatures living in it beneath the surface.

To clear the water jump, you need to take a slight diversion off a corner of the track and across a small muddy stretch. I ran right up to the jump before producing another side-step, shaking my head as I passed by. This caused some consternation, both with the water-jump officials and with the nearby spectators. This *mzungu* was clearly not going to win the race, but he was providing some entertainment.

I don't know what the other finalists thought of all this. I had a chance to ask them, as they lapped me for the first time after three laps, but they were past me in a flash, a wave of Kenyan legs eating up the track, leaving a plodding Englishman to his own devices.

Midway through the fourth lap, I began to develop stomach cramps. This was a potential disaster. I knew I was at altitude, but I expected to be able to run eight laps of the track. I changed my breathing pattern, inhaling and exhaling heavily after each stride. For a while it was pretty painful and my screwed-up face revealed my discomfort.

'Come on, you can do it!' someone shouted from the crowd. 'Go, English, go!' said someone else. 'Don't die on us!' another wag yelled, to surrounding merriment. 'Come on, Ian!' cried out the Puma team's cameraman.

The other finalists surged past me again during the sixth lap. This time I noticed they took longer. Some were struggling behind – but they did not really know the meaning of struggling. I was way ahead in that department. As I ran past the VIP stand I heard further shouts of encouragement. This spurred me on. Looking around the track, with two laps to go, I realised I was now out on my own. Everyone else had finished the race.

At this point the crowd seemed to unite in support. The pains in my stomach disappeared and as I began to pick up a little speed, so I started to enjoy myself. It became a wonderful, beautiful three minutes. The people of Kapsabet could see I was no athlete, at least no serious athlete, but they also recognised that I was trying my best. That was good enough for them. Their pure love of athletics meant, as I was told later, that they respected anyone who gave it a go, even me.

Sporting life

Answer booklet

First name

____

Last name

____

Write your answers in this booklet

Questions 1–7 are about *What a sports nutritionist does* (pages 3–4 in the Reading booklet).

1 In paragraph 1, Helga says she's an "educator". From paragraph 1, give one job that she does.

____

(1 mark)

2 According to paragraph 3, why do people not understand about diet? Tick one answer from the list below that you think is correct.

People don't understand about food because:	Tick one box
They aren't very clever.	
They aren't told the right things.	
They are looking for easy ways of improving their diets.	
They don't like eating proper food.	

(1 mark)

3 According to the information boxes about protein and carbohydrate, what should endurance athletes like marathon runners eat more of before and after a race? For each, explain one reason why.

When?	What endurance athletes should eat.	Why endurance athletes should eat more of it.
Before a race.		
After a race.		

(2 marks)

4 Here are three sub-headings which could be used for different sections of this text. Number each from 1–3 to show the order they should be placed in the text.

Sub-heading	Number
Counselling athletes	
A diet for each sport	
Speaking and writing	

(1 mark)

5 Give one reason why the writer has included quotations from Helga, a sports nutritionist.

- ____

____

(1 mark)

6 From the *Carbohydrate loading* box, explain the different reasons why the following words and phrases are in inverted commas in the text: "hit the wall", "carbohydrate loading" and "tricks".
Complete the table with one different explanation for each word or phrase.

	The use of inverted commas
"hit the wall"	
"carbohydrate loading"	
"tricks"	

(3 marks)

7 What qualities does the text suggest someone would need for Helga's job? Support each answer with a quotation from the text.

- ____

____

- ____

____

____

(2 marks)

Questions 8–13 are about *Off the beaten track* (pages 5–6 in the Reading booklet).

8 What does the title (*Off the beaten track*) suggest about this holiday?

- ____

(1 mark)

9 According to paragraph 4, what two types of mountain biking does the island offer?

- ____
- ____

(1 mark)

10 In the *Off the beaten track* section, how does the writer's use of language try to persuade the reader to choose this holiday?

You should comment on

- descriptions he uses
- the style of the writing
- the way he addresses the reader.

- ____

(5 marks)

11 **a** Paragraph 6 suggests that not everyone who goes on this holiday is there for the cycling. According to the information in the *Nidri: A typical week*, give one day on which cyclists would be able to spend time with non-cycling friends.

• ______________________________

(1 mark)

b Explain why they will be able to spend time together.

• ______________________________

____

(1 mark)

12 The *Nidri: A typical week* section contains much of the same information as Off the beaten track. Explain one reason for including the *Nidri: A typical week* section.

• ______________________________

____

(1 mark)

13 What differences are there in the way the two sections are organised? Complete the following table.

Section	**Organisation**
Off the beaten track	
Nidri: A typical week	

(2 marks)

Questions 14–16 are about *The race of my life* (pages 7–8 in the Reading booklet).

14 According to paragraph 2, what two sports has the writer played recently?

- ______________________________
- ______________________________

(1 mark)

15 How does the structure of the paragraphs help the reader to follow the events? Complete the following tables.

a Look at **Paragraph 6 and 7**. Identify one word or phrase from paragraph 7 that makes a link between paragraph 6 and 7. Explain the link.

Word/phrase	Explanation of the link

b Look at **Paragraph 8**. Explain how the information in the paragraph links with the first sentence.

Paragraph 8 topic sentence.	How the content of the paragraph links with the topic sentence.
"The water jump was always going to provide the major point of interest."	

c Look at **Paragraph 13**. The writer describes different parts of the race. In the box below, underline two phrases the writer uses to signal the sequence of events.

> "The other finalists surged past me again during the sixth lap. This time I noticed they took longer. Some were struggling behind – but they did not really know the meaning of struggling. I was way ahead in that department. As I ran past the VIP stand I heard further shouts of encouragement. This spurred me on. Looking around the track, with two laps to go, I realised I was now out on my own. Everyone else had finished the race."

(3 marks)

16 Explain the writer's attitude towards his performance in the race.

You should comment on:

- how he prepared for the race
- how he describes the crowd reacting to his performance
- how he felt about his performance during the race.

(5 marks)

Assessment focuses for the questions

		AF2 Describe, select or retrieve information, events or ideas from texts and use quotation and reference to text.	AF3 Deduce, infer or interpret information, events or ideas from texts.	AF4 Identify and comment on the structure and organisation of texts, including grammatical and presentational features at text level.	AF5 Comment on writers' uses of language, including grammatical and literary features at word and sentence level.	AF6 Identify and comment on writers' purposes and viewpoints, and the effect of the text on the reader.	
What a sports nutritionist does	1	1					
	2	1					
	3		2				
	4			1			
	5					1	
	6				3		
	7		2				
	Total	**2**	**4**	**1**	**3**	**1**	**11**
Off the beaten track	8				1		
	9	1					
	10				5		
	11		2				
	12					1	
	13			2			
	Total	**1**	**2**	**2**	**6**	**1**	**12**
The race of my life	14	1					
	15			3			
	16					5	
	Total	**1**	**0**	**3**	**0**	**5**	**9**
	Total	**4**	**6**	**5**	**9**	**7**	**32**

Growing pains

Reading Booklet

Growing pains

Contents

Growing up can be an experience filled with difficulties and challenges. It can be a time of conflict with problems with bullies or disagreements with parents. Growing up can also happen too quickly as can be seen in the cases of children who are forced to start work at a young age.

Growing pains

This text is from a novel, Dance with a Poor Man's Daughter by Pamela Jooste, set in South Africa. Here Lily recalls an incident when a local gang, led by Portia, pushed her into a water trough.

Fighting against the bullies

Portia tells one of the boys to run over to the trough and fill up one of the glass jars Andries keeps there for carrying water to the graves. You can see the boy is scared of her because although the pebbles must have burned his feet, he is quick as lightning and when he gives her the full jar and water is splashing all over the place, she throws it all over me so my dress is soaking wet and she laughs and says it's only water and it won't kill me and everyone thinks it's a big joke.

She knows I can't get away and I know it too and so I stand quite still while they move closer to me and my heart is beating so hard you can see it pushing up and down right through my dress.

Then Portia makes up her mind and says they should push me right into the trough and they start pushing me, so that one of my sandals falls off my foot and one of the boys is tugging at my shoulders and it feels as though they're pulling my arms almost out of their sockets and that hurts and it's not funny and then I'm sitting on the edge of the trough and kicking out with my legs as hard as I can but I can't keep my balance.

I know what's going to happen but I can't do anything about it. I topple backwards and my shoulders hit the water and someone gets hold of me from behind and pushes hard, so that the cold water closes over my head and bangs my eyes closed and tiny, slimy fronds of waterweed swirl around my face.

My nose is blocked and I go under in such a hurry I forget to breathe and I kick as hard as I can but a hundred hands seem to be pulling at me and I can hear them shouting and myself gasping for air before I go under again and I can hear the flap of water in my ears and a rush of bubbles drowns their voices.

I think I am going to drown and my hair floats over my face like tough little snakes and the water pulls at the skirt of my dress.

I know them when they get like this. They'll go on and on until they get tired and it isn't fun any more.

I try to loose my hand so I can pull myself out. I kick back as hard

continued

continued

as I can but it's no good because no matter how hard I pull and kick I can't do it hard enough and there are more of them and only one of me.

I want to scream but I am under the water and when I open my mouth air bubbles out of it and dirty water pours in and there's nothing I can do. I'm going to drown and all that worries me is that my grandmother will have to fetch my body from the police station fridge and go with my coffin on the train to Maitland Cemetery.

Portia and her gang won't care. They'll leave me there, heavy as a stone, at the bottom of the trough with streamers of slime floating across me, in and out of my hair and my mind is full of these thoughts and how happy they will be and that makes me angry.

I don't care that I'm lying under that water and they're pushing me down. I make up my mind they can do anything they like to me but they needn't feel too happy about it because I don't really mind as much as they think I do, so they have no reason to get excited and full of themselves about it and act as if they are kings of the castle.

They can do what they like to me and if I make up my mind I can tell myself I don't mind at all. It may even suit me. They may even be doing me a favour.

So I stop kicking and lie still under the water which, at least is cool and I'm not sure what will happen next, but if so many people have drowned before now without any problems then it can't be all that difficult to do. Especially once you've made up your mind about it.

Then it's over. I hear shouting and someone pulls at me and there are bubbles and splashes and I am being pulled out of the water and the sun is almost blinding me and old Andries is shouting at Portia and her gang.

Growing pains

This text is from a newspaper advice column written by the journalist Virginia Ironside. Here she is responding to a problem that has been sent to her by a parent who is concerned about her children's appearances.

DILEMMA

THIS WEEKS PROBLEM

Marina has a problem with her children's appearances. Her 14-year-old son is planning to get a ring through his nose, with or without his parent's permission; her 12-year-old daughter wears mini-skirts so short her bottom shows. Marina wants to give them their freedom but she doesn't know how far she should go

Adolescent children are fantastically self conscious about their appearance. They'll wear nothing that isn't dead right for their crowd. That's why, if you buy them a green jersey of the wrong green, or a pair of socks covered with musical notes that you think are 'fun' and they think are naff, they often simply refuse to wear them.

So when Marina's children decide to take certain design decisions, she can be certain that in their own circle they'll look absolutely spot on. She may think they look weird, their friends will think they look the bee's knees.

The fact that *she* thinks they look provocative or brutal is beside the point. Who cares what adults think? A gang of skinheads is hardly likely to pounce on a boy just because of a ring in his nose; they'll have far more sympathy with Marina's young son than Marina herself. In the sixties, I was one of the first to wear mini skirts, long black boots and fish-net stockings. The look shrieked 'tart' in a far louder voice then than any mini-skirt from Jigsaw would today. Nothing ever happened to me because of my clothes.

Marina must remember not only her own teenage whims but also how irritating it was when her children begged her not to wear certain things to pick them up from school. 'Oh, Mum, you look so weird in those funny trousers ...' was the wail from my son when I went a bit mad on some ghastly, never to be worn again breeches.

But as we, as parents, tone down our dress when in the company of our children and their friends to save them dreadful embarrassment, it's quite right that our children should do the same when around our contemporaries – or their grandparents. Longer skirts. Nose-ring temporarily removed. But, generally, dress is a harmless way of expressing individuality. If Marina forces her kids into V-necked jumpers and clean jeans, their individuality will only express itself in other, far more dangerous ways. Neat as pins on the outside; probably stoned to the eyebrows on the inside.

Marina can express her anxieties, but after that she should shut up as she starts to practise the difficult new 'hands off' parenting of the adolescent. 'It's only a phase,' she can remind herself. Only too soon, sadly, her children are going to look pretty much exactly the same as all the other young men and women in the street.

Text 3 Growing pains

This text is from a magazine article about child labour. The article tells the story of Kumar, a young boy from Nepal who runs away from home.

Kumar's story

Kumar Subba left his village home in eastern Nepal at the age of eight. He crept out of his house before dawn and walked 30 kilometres to a small country town. He was escaping a family catastrophe. His father, a peasant farmer, had lost his land to a local moneylender and left for India to look for work. While his mother laboured for a pittance in other people's fields, Kumar was trapped at home minding younger brothers and sisters.

When I left my only thought was to escape. I got a job in a hotel. I had to fetch water and wash the dishes. The water was icy. Sometimes I was sent to a nearby forest to collect firewood. I was not paid – just given two meals a day. I slept on the tables after the customers left. I got bad sores on my hands and fell sick. Sick or well, I had to work.

After a year, I left and walked to the next town where I worked as a street porter, living on the streets. But the older boys would bully and rob us. One day a man told me he could get me a job in Kathmandu. I would be trained to weave carpets and have a chance to go to school. I would be given very good meals. Once trained, I would earn a lot of money. I saved for six months for the bus fare to Kathmandu. But this agent was another cheat.

The factory he took me to was very big and full of working children, mostly girls. It was like a prison. We were locked in. I was ten years old but not the youngest. We worked from 5.00am to midnight knotting carpets. We slept among the looms. Many of the children suffered pains in their fingers because of the work. We were given very low-quality rice and thin watery lentils twice a day. Those were the only breaks and no-one spoke of paying us.

Supervisors checked that we didn't fall asleep. They also had informers among us who would report us if we fought or broke the hammers, needles or scissors we used. Then we would be thrashed. There was some bullying though not as bad as on the streets.

When others slept some of us would talk about how we landed up there and the promises made us. We had all been cheated by the labour contractors.

After six months I was exhausted and had pains in my hands, stomach and chest. One day, I spotted a half-broken window in the lavatory. I broke out and ran away.

After that I worked as a ragpicker and slept on the streets. It was better than the factory – at least you could have some fun. Other young children taught me where to collect rags and sell them. There were also older boys who were into pickpocketing and thieving. They ordered me to strip valuable metals from buildings. If I refused I was beaten.

The worst thing on the streets was that nobody treated us well and everyone, police and other adults, all behaved like thieves and cheats. We were often arrested and beaten or tortured for no reason. The police kicked or beat us with special ribbed sticks; sometimes we were bound by ropes and beaten. At first I was very innocent but then I thought: 'Whether I steal or not, I get arrested and beaten; better get beaten with thieving than without.' So I started stealing things as well.

I ended up being jailed for six months and put in a cell with adults, including a monitor chosen by the prison staff. Everyone had to make him happy because if he reported you to the warders you lost your right to parole. The warders also let him beat you up. You had to make tea for the adults and wash their clothes.

Back on the street, I was the youngest of a group who were getting seriously into thieving. Some would even take on security guards who caught them in the act. One day I had a head injury. My friends took me to the health clinic at Child Workers in Nepal.

There, for the first time, I found adults who cared about me and shared things with me. I stayed on in a night shelter they have and got involved in their activities. That was in 1992, so I was 11.

Increasingly recognized as a talented artist, Kumar – now 16 – plans to be both a painter and street educator so that he can help other working children realize some of their aspirations. He has also been reconciled with his family.

Growing pains

Answer booklet

First name

____

Last name

____

Write your answers in this booklet

Questions 1–6 are about *Fighting against the bullies* (pages 3–4 in the Reading booklet)

1 From paragraph 1, explain one way the writer shows that the gang are afraid of Portia.

- ______________________________

____

(1 mark)

2 According to paragraph 2, what does the way Lily responds to the water show about her attitude towards Portia? Support your answer with a quotation.

- ______________________________

____

(1 mark)

3 How does the writer's use of language in paragraphs 4–6 make the experience of being pushed under the water sound horrible? Identify one quotation from each and explain each of them.

Quotation	How it makes the experience sound horrible
Paragraph 4:	
Paragraph 5:	
Paragraph 6:	

(3 marks)

4 According to paragraph 11, explain one motive Portia and her gang have for bullying Lily.

- ______________________________

____

____

(1 mark)

5 The writer uses the present tense and long sentences to describe this incident. Give one effect on the reader of the way this story is told.

- ____________________

(1 mark)

6 In the section from "I think I'm going to drown" to the end of the text, how does the writer build up the seriousness of the attack?

You should comment on:

- the comments Lily makes at the beginning of this section and her efforts to save herself
- how Lily persuades herself that she will drown
- how this section ends.

- ____________________

(5 marks)

Questions 7–12 are about *Dilemma* (page 5 in the Reading booklet).

7 From paragraph 2, give one fashion error that the writer says parents might make.

• ______________________________

(1 mark)

8 Explain two ways that the writer's use of language in paragraphs 2 and 3 shows her support of the children's point of view. Support each answer with a quotation from the text.

• ______________________________

____

____

• ______________________________

____

____

(2 marks)

9 In paragraph 4 and 5, the writer includes details about herself. What is the purpose of doing this? Explain two reasons.

• ______________________________

____

• ______________________________

____

(2 marks)

10 In paragraph 5, what does the writer suggest about teenage dress sense in the phrase "teenage whims"?

Teenage whims suggests that: • ______________________________

____

(1 mark)

11 How is paragraph 6 organised to persuade Marina and other parents to follow the writer's advice? Complete the table:

Information from paragraph 6	How the organisation persuades Marina
But as we, as parents, tone down our dress when in the company of our children and their friends to save them dreadful embarrassment, it's quite right that our children should do the same when around our contemporaries – or their grandparents. Longer skirts. Nose-ring temporarily removed.	
But, generally, dress is a harmless way of expressing individuality.	
If Marina forces her kids into V-necked jumpers and clean jeans, their individuality will only express itself in other, far more dangerous ways. Neat as pins on the outside; probably stoned to the eyebrows on the inside.	

(3 marks)

12 In the final sentence, *"Only too soon, sadly, her children are going to look pretty much exactly the same as all the other young men and women in the street"* what do you think the writer means when she says they will all look the same?

- ______________________________

____

(1 mark)

Answer booklet

Questions 13–16 are about *Kumar's story* (pages 6–7 in the Reading booklet).

13 Explain one way that the writer's language in the first paragraph makes the reader feel sympathetic towards Kumar.

- ____

____

(1 mark)

14 In paragraph 3, what different impressions do you get of Kumar? Complete the following table by writing down two more quotations and explaining what each quotation suggests about Kumar.

Quotation	What the quotation suggests about the character of Kumar
"I would be trained to weave carpets and have a chance to go to school"	

(3 marks)

15 According to paragraph 9, why did Kumar start stealing?

- ____

____

(1 mark)

16 This text was written by Anthony Swift, based on an interview with Kumar, and was published with other information about child labour. Explain the writer's purposes in writing this text.

You should comment on:

- the things Kumar says about how he was treated at work.
- the problems Kumar faced on the streets
- Kumar since his accident and rescue.
-

(5 marks)

Assessment focuses for the questions

		AF2 Describe, select or retrieve information, events or ideas from texts and use quotation and reference to text.	**AF3** Deduce, infer or interpret information, events or ideas from texts.	**AF4** Identify and comment on the structure and organisation of texts, including grammatical and presentational features at text level.	**AF5** Comment on writers' uses of language, including grammatical and literary features at word and sentence level.	**AF6** Identify and comment on writers' purposes and viewpoints, and the effect of the text on the reader.	
Fighting against the bullies	**1**	1					
	2		1				
	3				3		
	4		1				
	5					1	
	6			5			
	Total	**1**	**2**	**5**	**3**	**1**	**12**
Dilemma	**7**	1					
	8				2		
	9					2	
	10				1		
	11			3			
	12		1				
	Total	**1**	**1**	**3**	**3**	**2**	**10**
Kumar's story	**13**				1		
	14		3				
	15	1					
	16					5	
	Total	**1**	**3**	**0**	**1**	**5**	**10**
	Total	**3**	**6**	**8**	**7**	**8**	**32**